T0062423

# In Sunshine

and

# In Shadow:

## A Memoir

Muriel Tomkins Niemi

Order this book online at www.trafford.com
or email orders@trafford.com

Most Trafford titles are also available at major online book retailers.

Printed in Victoria, BC, Canada.

ISBN: 978-1-4251-9060-6 (soft)
ISBN: 978-1-4251-9062-0 (ebook)

*Our mission is to efficiently provide the world's finest, most comprehensive
book publishing service, enabling every author to experience success.
To find out how to publish your book, your way, and have it available
worldwide, visit us online at www.trafford.com*

*Trafford rev. 12/10/2009*

Trafford PUBLISHING®   www.trafford.com

**North America & international**
toll-free: 1 888 232 4444 (USA & Canada)
phone: 250 383 6864 ♦ fax: 812 355 4082

To My Beloved

# Chapter 1

YESTERDAY I visited my father's grave atop Mount Royal, high above the city of Montreal, where I was born in 1922. The grave bears a simple marker, placed there by the veterans' association. It reads:

*George S. Tomkins*
*Sergeant*
*23 Res. Battn. C.E.F.*
*2 Apr 1957 Age 76*

"C.E.F." refers to the Canadian Expeditionary Force in which my father fought during World War I. Next to the marker is a shiny pinkish-beige marble headstone that bears the inscription:

*STANLEY*
*Peace, perfect peace*

Stanley, my mother's brother, died in 1900, and was the first occupant of the grave. I was amazed to see that, after more than a hundred years, the stone is in nearly perfect condition. It has survived the lashing of snow and ice storms during the long, freezing Montreal winters and the suffocating heat and humidity of Montreal summers. The story of Stanley is a touching one. He was the third of seven children—three girls and four boys, one of whom died in infancy. Stanley was only fourteen when he died. It was his long-time habit to ride the cow-catcher of the train that passed near his home. On this occasion, his leg became somehow caught in the mechanism and was cut off. He is said to have instructed his rescuers to bring his severed leg, "because it has a new shoe on it." He survived only a few days. Little was known then about the effects of shock and its treatment with blood plasma and other remedies. My grandfather was told that he should sue the railway, and his reply was "No, it won't bring Stanley back."

Evidently Stanley was a terrific kid. He was loved by everyone, including the local butcher, who vowed that, when Stanley recovered, he could have a place for life in the butcher's prosperous shop.

In those days, because of the hard frozen ground, the coffins of people who died in the winter were stored in cement structures awaiting the spring. So it was with Stanley. When spring came, and Stanley was to be buried in the ground, my grandfather could not resist the temptation to look once more on the face of his beloved son. I think he regretted that action. Evidently Stanley's face was sunken, his hair had grown very long, and his fingernails had reached grotesque lengths, so that his hands resembled claws.

In subsequent years, the grave filled up with the cremated remains of my grandparents, my mother's older sister, and, finally, my father.

As I looked at the gently undulating grass of the cemetery, I noticed a variety of memorials. I have always been moved by the sweetly sad sight of the small square stones that usually denote a child's death. Then there are the towering cement crosses, an angel brooding over a grave, a statue of Jesus, and many great and small headstones scattered across the landscape. Here and there, a grey stone mausoleum peeks out from behind a clump of trees. When we were young, we would press our noses against the grillwork and shout, enjoying the echoes of our voices as they reverberated through the narrow vault. Then we would run like mad, certain that the disturbed spirits were in hot pursuit. The mausolea, with their stained glass windows, hinted at the opulence in which their inhabitants had once lived.

But cemeteries are not only peaceful places, with their green lawns, lush trees, and quiet paths. Cemeteries are great levellers, equalizers, cautioning us that not power, beauty, wealth, or talent saves anyone from the grave. Also, they are pieces of social history. For example, in three Halifax, Nova Scotia, cemeteries are the graves of 150 victims of the sinking of the mighty *Titanic*. They bear mute testimony to the tragedy that claimed over 1500 lives in the icy waters of the North Atlantic on April 15, 1912.

As these thoughts coursed through my mind, I found myself reflecting on the extraordinary events of my father's life. He was born in Salisbury, England, in the shadow of the great cathedral, in 1881, the only son of his parents, who also produced four girls. When he was six months old, the family emigrated to Chicago, Illinois, part of a swelling population that left the Old World for the New in search of opportunity. The family settled in Park Ridge, a small prairie town on the outskirts of Chicago, now a bustling suburb. There is little in the way of family records of this period, but the Chicago Historical Society librarian produced a school program for the year 1891, in which the graduation ceremony was presided over by my paternal grandfather, Edmund Ewing Tomkins, as Chairman of the School Board. The program indicates that my father did a recitation, and that his sister Lucy played the piano.

Thanks to my niece's interest in genealogy, we have been able to piece together the course of my father's adventurous life. How I wish I had questioned him about those events! Too often, we are so absorbed in the present that we fail to confer with our parents, grandparents, and other relatives about the events of their lives. And too few of them keep the letters, journals, diaries, and photograph albums that are fruitful sources of family history, capturing both the substance and the spirit of the times in which they were produced.

At various times, my father served in the American Army (though he remained a British subject all of his life), fought in the Boer War at the turn of the century at the age of seventeen, joined the Northwest Mounted Police in Canada, and enlisted in the British Grenadier Guards. In the latter capacity, he was present at the pomp and ceremony attending Queen Victoria's funeral in 1901. I have a vision of him as a young Grenadier Guard, tall, erect, resplendent in his scarlet dress uniform topped by the towering, bushy bearskin that became a hallmark of the Guards. It was a memorable event in that it brought together, for the last time, the many crowned heads of Europe. Few people realized that, within a few years, most of these rulers would be deposed, driven into exile, or, like Tsar Nicholas II of Russia, murdered.

I believe that I inherited my father's adventurous spirit and his love of martial music. To this day, the beat of a marching band and the wild skirl of bagpipes, set my heart dancing.

I am not certain of the circumstances under which my father returned to Canada in 1916. World War I was underway, and he wanted to be part of the action. He travelled to Montreal to enlist in the Canadian Expeditionary Force (C.E.F.). What happened there is the stuff of romance. He walked into the West End Branch of the Bank of Montreal, saw my mother, and fell instantly, like David Copperfield, into "an abyss of love," in which he was to remain for the rest of his life. He liked to recall that she had long black hair tied with a red ribbon and that she wore a white blouse and a long black skirt. The sight must have been enchanting, for, only the day before, the bank manager had exclaimed, "Miss Staines, you look like a painting by Gainsborough," the famous portrait artist.

I am looking at a picture of my mother taken some years earlier, when she was about ten years old. She is sitting upright on a chair, wearing a white lace dress and black stockings. Her long black hair flows loosely about her shoulders. Her large eyes look straight ahead and her expression is pleasant and serious, not quite as grim as faces usually are in old photographs. I once asked my mother why people looked so grim in old photographs, and she replied, "They look grim because, in those days, taking a photograph involved a long, laborious process. The photographer had to mount his camera on a tripod, cover the camera and his head with a large black cloth, adjust the lens, and wait for the right moment." Beside her in the photograph is a handsome oak library table with tooled legs, on which was displayed a massive family Bible almost a foot high. Underneath her feet is a carpet strewn with huge cabbage roses. So thoroughly Victorian is the picture that it almost looks contrived.

After a brief courtship, my father left to fight in France, but not before bestowing on my mother an engagement ring, which I have. It features a pink cameo set in gold and flanked with diamonds. She was seventeen, and he was 35 years old, more than twice her age. He was gone for two years, during which they corresponded faithfully and she knitted socks for him and sent him parcels of cookies. Most of his letters and cards became lost over the years during many moves, but a few survive. Invariably, they ended with the letters "T.T.D.", heavily underlined. Those letters stood for "True Till Death."

In 1917, my father fought at Passchendaele in Belgium. It is said that, upon viewing the site, Sir Douglas Haig's Chief of Staff, Lieutenant General Sir Launcelot Kiggell, exclaimed, "My God, did we send men into that?" Tim Cook, in his book entitled No Place to Run, described the scene vividly: "Millions of shells and constant rain had churned the ground into viscous mud that devoured material, men, and horses." According to the World War 1 Databook by John Ellis and Michael Cox (Aurum Press Limited, London, 2001) casualties at Passchendaele (often called the Third Battle of Ypres) totalled 306,800, including 60,300 dead. My father told me about an incident that happened at Passchendaele. He pulled out a man who was drowning in the slimy mud. A few years later, my father encountered this man on a Montreal street, but the man was behaving erratically and didn't recognize my father.

My father was hit by a shell and sustained a shattered left knee. Also, he suffered mustard gas attacks by the Germans. Not surprisingly, he was glad to be wounded, because he escaped the horrors of the mud, the trenches, and the gas warfare, and he was at last able to sleep in a bed with clean sheets. His knee healed, but the injury left him with a permanent limp. Today, no doubt, he would have had a knee replacement, a technique that was unknown at that time.

In the meantime, my mother was entertaining serious doubts about whether she should go ahead with this marriage. She had made her vow to my father two years earlier in the spirit of romance and high idealism that prevailed before and during World War I. It was "the war to end all wars" and "the war to make the world safe for democracy." But she was a child of the Victorian Age, when people were imbued with a strong sense of duty. Whether you liked it or not, you kept your promises. Thus, on December 10, 1918, when my father returned from the war, Winifred Audrey Staines and George Strong Tomkins were married and moved into the first of several cold-water flats that they would occupy in Montreal for a very long time. My brother (named "George," after our father, but always called "Tom" by the family) was born in 1920, and I was born two years later.

The relationship between my parents was somewhat strained, although I never heard them exchange an angry word. My father adored my mother. For her part, I think she felt that her early doubts had been confirmed, but she decided to make the best of it. I don't believe that my father noticed her attitude. Perhaps he didn't want to notice it. Another aspect of the relationship between my parents was that my father was happy to leave all the decisions to my mother, who was happy to take charge. She was one of those small, fragile-looking women who are about as fragile as bulldozers. It must be admitted that, under more favourable economic conditions, my mother might have sought a divorce, but she had lacked the skills needed to support herself and two children. In any event, divorce was frowned upon and, for that reason, was rare. Perhaps, as things turned out, it was well that my parents did not separate. Thus, Tom and I enjoyed a degree of emotional security that eludes many of today's children. We knew, with certainty, that our parents would stay together and that they would look after us. As for our own relationship, like most siblings, we often vied with each other for our parents' attention and quarrelled over other matters as well. There was just one occasion when a quarrel turned violent, and I long ago forgot the reason. I vividly remember stabbing him with the pointed end of a long-handled paint brush. He retaliated by tossing a tin can that grazed my head. Like most head wounds, this one bled profusely, and I enjoyed the drama of a few hours when my hair dried and became matted with blood. My secret hope was that I would die and he would be forced to spend the rest of his life in sackcloth and ashes. Actually, he was horrified at his own action, for he was by nature rather gentle. I, too, was horrified by my action. "Look what you've done to your sister," my father, ever protective of me, cried, and Tom retreated in horror from this misdeed. The matter was never mentioned again by Tom or me. On another occasion when we quarrelled, I accused Tom of being a "pimp." I had no idea what the term meant, only that it was derogatory! My parents heard this accusation, and their faces were a study. What to do! To explain the term was to invoke that dreaded taboo word "sex." To laugh, as they were tempted to do, would give a kind of tacit validation to the term. So they said nothing, and it was a long time before I learned the meaning of the word "pimp."

Another aspect of my parents' relationship was my father's jealousy, occasioned, perhaps, by the disparity in their ages. My father's jealousy extended to Tom, whom my mother adored. This circumstance caused my father to exhibit harsh behaviour toward Tom, attacking him for small transgressions, while excusing me for larger ones. His jealousy also manifested itself whenever my father's wartime buddy, John McColl, came to dinner. My father would demand of my mother, "You like him, don't you?" My mother never answered. Actually, it was my father's idea that John McColl should be invited to dinner often.

Although Tom and I tired of his visits, I am glad, in ret-rospect, that we had him regularly, as he lived in a small, miserable, one-room apartment on a shabby street near McGill University, and he had no other friends or rela-tives. He was one of those hapless people who seem to invite misfortune. He hadn't been home from the war for more than two months when he bought a new overcoat to shield himself from the bitterly cold Montreal winters. He wore it for the first time when he went to a restaurant for dinner. When he had finished, and went to retrieve his coat, it was gone, replaced by an old, shabby coat that had seen much wear. Some years later, he developed tu-berculosis and was sent to a sanitorium in the Laurentian Mountains, where he died at the age of 69.

Like so many others of his generation, John McColl had little education and few skills. Thus he was des-tined to sit at a work bench in an electrical company's plant and pound nails into small appliances. He had an air of patient resignation. "I shot my bolt in the war," he said. He, too, was injured. A bullet hit him in the mouth, causing his lips to be deformed and many teeth to be de-stroyed. Once he told my mother that he had met a girl in Edinburgh during the war. "The sun never shone so brightly," he said, "and the birds never sang so sweetly." When my mother questioned him, "John, why don't you go back there and find her? Maybe she's missing you as much as you are missing her," he replied quietly, "Winnie, I have nothing to offer her." He returned to his work bench, and continued pounding nails into small appliances.

I don't know whether anyone has studied the chil-dren who were born to veterans of World War I, the most widespread conflict in history until that time. Tom and I were afraid of our father. Our earliest memories were of his screaming during nightmares that were almost certainly inspired by the horrors of Passchendaele. When this happened, I would cover my ears and shiver in bed. Also, he would fly into unpredictable rages over trivial matters. Each year, for some time after the war, my father manifested the symptoms of someone suffering from a gas attack. They took the form of red streaming eyes, a streaming nose, and some coughing fits. I never knew whether the condition was psychological or physiological. Perhaps it was a bit of both. There is nothing as futile as regret, but I find myself thinking that he needed much love, understanding, and support, and regretting that we withheld it from him.

He struggled to be a good father and he was certainly a good provider. It seemed to me that my father, John McColl, and countless others exemplified the words that Erich Maria Remarque wrote in his brief preface to <u>All Quiet on the Western Front</u>, the famous war novel written from the standpoint of a German soldier. The preface to the novel reads: "It will try simply to tell of a generation of men who, though they may have escaped its shells, were destroyed by the war."

The veterans returning from World War I found a nation ill-prepared to ease their transition to civilian life. The bewildered veterans received only sporadic help with housing, education, health and counselling. Morton and Wright reported in <u>Winning the Second Battle</u> (1987) that "from the case files there is much evidence of hardship that was not relieved, and of claims that were not met." They also reported that "fifteen years after the war, 77,000 veterans collected disability pensions, while thousands more endured pain, debility, or premature aging without going through the sometimes humiliating ordeal of establishing a claim." My father was lucky to find a job in the Montreal Post Office, where he remained for 25 years before retiring. I have often marvelled at his fortitude in staying on the job, considering that he had lived such an adventurous life. One of his sisters exclaimed to my mother, "How did you ever keep him in one place for 25 years?" Having fought on three continents, there he was, reduced to the mind-numbing task of sorting mail destined for the cities, towns, and rural areas of the Province of Quebec. A major difficulty was that the overwhelming majority of postal workers were French, and my father neither spoke nor understood the language. I can see him now, going to work with a sandwich stuffed in his pocket and a nickel for a cup of coffee. He looked so shabby that, on one occasion, a stranger gave him a dollar.

I have always felt badly about my parents' generation. They were plunged early into World War I (called the "Great War" at that time) that began with high idealism as "the war to end wars" and culminated in a slaughter and an uneasy peace. There followed the bitter Depression and, then, a second world war, a scant 25 years after the first. At the start of that war, my mother was 40 and my father was 58. He never earned more than $150.00 per month, a sum that was cut in half when he retired on pension (and cut in half again for my mother after his death.) Once again, they were plunged into penury, struggling to pay their bills. They never rode the economic boom that followed the end of the war. As I watched my mother scrimping, saving, doing without, and scrubbing clothes on a washboard, and knew that she had not welcomed children because my parents couldn't afford them, I made a silent resolve never to get into that fix. Never. I might add that contraception was unreliable and even frowned upon by many people, the pill was unknown, and abortions were illegal.

It has been said, concerning the era in which I grew up, that since everyone around us was poor, we didn't realize that we were poor. It was true that we were not what has been called "dirt poor," but we lived very close to the edge. The constant struggle to provide food for the table every day occupied too much of our thoughts. I recall, in particular, the acute anxiety that beset my parents as another payday approached. Would our money last until then? I remember clearly that the news that Tom required a $5.00 history text in Grade 11 created a near-crisis for them. Because they believed in education, there was never any real doubt that the text would be purchased.

Then there was the ever-looming possibility that my father would be laid off in an era where there was no employment insurance. There was welfare, called "relief," but it was minimal, and many families were ashamed to accept relief, because it signified that their men could not support them. I could sense my mother's terror, which was almost palpable, at the prospect of my father losing his job. Indeed, it happened several times. On the very day that my mother returned from the hospital with their newborn son, my father was laid off. Their latent fear was that these temporary layoffs might become permanent. As a small child, I reflected this fear and tried to comfort them and myself. It was reported to me that one day I opened the ice-box door and announced, "Well, we have lots of eggs and jam!"

To this day, although I am comfortably off by a modest standard, I still entertain an unreasonable fear that perhaps my money won't see me through. I find myself economizing in rather ridiculous ways. For instance, I rarely treat myself to lunch or dinner at a restaurant more than once a week, on the grounds that it would be extravagant. As I write these words, I recall walking up a long, steep hill in Montreal on a blazing hot day, in order to save eight cents on carfare. The timeless adage that old habits die hard still holds. An important point I want to make is that the constant tension relating to money that permeated our lives sapped much of the joy that we should have experienced as a family.

We lived in a succession of cold-water flats in Ville Emard, Cote St. Paul, and Verdun. On many Verdun streets, there was a long, drab row of identical two-story flats that featured outside staircases leading to the second-floor flat. My chief memory of living in cold-water flats is that I was always cold. None of us really complained about being cold. It was simply an inescapable fact of life. The three flats we lived in had long halls from which the rooms branched off. There was a wood stove in the kitchen and, at the other end of the flat, was something called a "Quebec heater." This was a round iron stove resembling a barrel, and it supplied heat for a few feet in each direction.

As for taking a bath, the routine was to heat a kettle of hot water to boiling point, rush to the bathroom to pour the hot water into the bath and add an inch or two of cold water. The result was that we bathed in perhaps three inches of water at most. To this day, I luxuriate in and am grateful for generous hot water baths. There were no washing machines, and we washed everything by hand in a tub or in the kitchen sink, often using a corrugated wooden scrubbing board and yellow Sunlight soap so strong it made our nostrils twitch.

My mother ameliorated the drabness of the cold-water flats in which we lived with her touches of elegance, such as her small collection of china cups, a china dinner set, and some silver dishes. She was abetted by her father, who brought her heavily discounted items from Henry Morgan and Company, a stylish "carriage trade" store where he worked as Chief Accountant. Thus we enjoyed drinking tea from real china cups and saucers. I might add that, when my grandfather retired from Morgan's in 1932, he was handed a cheque for $1,000.00, a very large sum in those days. It was a striking testimony to the value of his services, all the more so because he was a self-educated man. My mother told me that, in his intense desire for education, he would hang on every word uttered by the local minister who, wonder of wonders, had a B.A. degree. She also told me that he spent long hours in the evening perfecting his handwriting.

Like her father, my mother was a quick learner. She taught herself to sew and became an excellent seamstress. She took old clothes that were given to her, washed them, turned them inside out, and created presentable, if not handsome clothes. I remember, in particular, a coat that she made for me out of an old coat that someone gave her. It was navy wool, and she trimmed it with black braid at the collar and cuffs. It was an attractive creation, and I wore it with pride. Her clothes and mine were always homemade, and I didn't buy any clothes until I was in my thirties.

My mother was also an excellent cook, who paid conscious attention to nutrition, though not much was known about it at that time. Thus, she saw to it that we had plenty of fruits and vegetables, oatmeal, milk, sometimes in the form of milk puddings which my father favoured, and so on.

As for shopping, it was the era of the corner grocery store, since replaced by the modern supermarket. It sold bread, milk, flour, sugar, canned goods, paper goods, and a few other items. There were biscuits in large square containers with glass lids, and we selected however many we wanted. Other items included sugar and salt sold by the pound, peanut butter in large pails, eggs in wooden crates, dill pickles in a barrel, and butter in waxed, wooden boxes.

There was a delirious moment, one summer day, when word got around that there was a new confection, ice cream, at the grocery store. Tom and I were dispatched to the store. I carried a large ceramic bowl, which I held out to be filled, like Oliver Twist asking for more gruel. The clerk filled the bowl with shiny scoops of frozen custard. We dashed home in great excitement to share this bounty. Several years later, my father bought an ice cream freezer. It consisted of a large, circular, light metal container in which a smaller container was set. The space between them was filled with cracked ice. I can still see my father patiently cranking away until the custard mixture in the smaller bowl hardened into ice cream.

Ice was delivered to our home every day from the large ice-house and stored quickly in the upper compartment of our ice-box. On very hot days, we waited with anxiety for the ice-man's visit, fearing that the food would spoil. In another sense, my mother hated the ice-man's visit, because he arrived with a huge, dripping, straw-encrusted block of ice, held in giant pincers. The kitchen floor was a mess. What a joy it was to welcome, much later, the arrival of our first refrigerator! Tom and I, out of our small salaries, each paid one-third of the cost.

More than a place to shop, the corner grocery store was a social center, especially for retired men in the community, particularly those living in small towns and in rural and semi-rural areas of Quebec. On cold winter days, it was common to see them clustered in hard wooden chairs around a huge, pot-bellied stove, gossiping, exchanging news, and swapping anecdotes. The practice led to the creation of a new term, "the Hot Stove League." I suspect that the league still exists and will continue to exist so long as there are small, locally owned grocery stores.

Another feature of life in our neighbourhood was the tiny corner candy store, a magnet for kids of my generation. The candy store contained a wondrous assortment of candy, including licorice pipes, licorice cigars, licorice plugs, jaw-breakers, all-day suckers, marshmallow strawberries and peanuts, jelly beans, maple buds, bubble gum, jujubes, chocolate-covered peanuts, humbugs, Sweet Marie bars and Cherry Delights. We would spend a long time in furious concentration, our noses pressed against the glass until they hurt. Always, inevitably, we chose the same item—a hard candy covered in chocolate called a "honeymoon." The reason? We could get two honeymoons for the large copper penny that was common in those days. If you were really rich—that is, if you managed to cadge fifteen cents from an indulgent relative—you could buy large dark chocolate bars studded with whole Brazil nuts.

Another magnet for us was the local bakery where, on Monday morning, one could buy a big brown bag full of smashed pastries for fifteen cents. It included fragments of cinnamon buns, broken jelly doughnuts, damaged Danishes in lemon and raspberry flavours, and small pieces of lemon pie that had become a gooey mess. But we thought the selection was wonderful—so much better than the homemade cakes and pies that our mothers sometimes created.

We had little in the way of recreation. Restaurants were scarce, and we couldn't have afforded to patronize them. Occasionally we would go for a picnic to a place called Stony Point in Lachine, a suburb of Montreal on Lake St. Louis. We awaited this event with great anticipation and great worry that the weather would spoil our plans. As we rattled along on the tram that took us to the picnic grounds, I squirmed at the scratchy texture of the black wool bathing suit I wore under a dress. Stony Point was well-named, for the lake was full of rocks of all sizes. It didn't matter because we couldn't swim. But we took pleasure in sunning ourselves on the rocks, splashing around in the water, and occasionally ducking each other. We were simply happy to get away from the hot city streets. A high point was our purchase of greasy french fries for a nickel from a nearby stand. To this day, I prefer soggy french fries over the crisp fries! Another excursion took us to Dominion Park, where we excitedly rode a rather ramshackle old roller coaster. It was a long trip on the slow-moving street car to the other side of Montreal, but we didn't mind, as it broke the rather dull routine of our daily lives. I am reminded of Moss Hart's remark in his autobiography, Act I: "Boredom is the keynote of poverty ... for where there is no money there is no change of any kind, not of scene or of routine."

Our boredom sometimes drove us to dangerous extremes. One escapade that we hid carefully from our parents, because they would have had fits, concerned our habit of making our way across the locks that spanned the nearby Lachine Canal. The locks consisted of narrow, wet, slippery planks of wood held together by low iron railings. We would cross the lock to the other side, stooping to the railings, turn around, and resume our perilous journey back. It never occurred to us that the slightest misstep would send us plunging into the waters of the canal below, and we couldn't swim. It was a heady adventure, and we were fearless.

Once or twice, we vacationed on farms within a short distance of the city. Many of these farms were dairy farms, where the owners made hay in the summer season and sold milk and butter to city folk. The farmer's wives supplemented their income by taking in summer boarders, and the four of us usually shared one large room. Typically, there was no bathroom, but an outhouse that featured large store catalogues. At first I assumed they were there for purposes of entertainment, but I soon discovered that the slippery pages had a more serious purpose. We ate with the family at a large square table in the kitchen. The meals were ordinary, and they always featured an array of pickled beets, corn relish, and cold stewed tomatoes. There was little to do on the farms, except go for walks, dodging the cow platters on the paths. Sometimes there would be an improvised swimming hole, where Tom and I enjoyed splashing in the cool water.

In the city, we spent much time on the street. There was no television and only limited radio reception. Our radio was housed in an enormous, carved, shiny wooden cabinet, standing at least four feet tall, and the reception was uncertain. What a contrast to today's compact iPod that fits into the palm of one's hand! So attached were Tom and I to certain programs, especially Sunday night programs, that we were reluctant to leave the house on those nights. We especially liked the Eddie Cantor Show and One Man's Family. I remember one show, in particular, that nearly scared Tom and me out of our wits and made us cower in our beds. It was called "Lights Out!" It was introduced by a sepulchral voice, as one emanating from a tomb, that intoned: "Lights out! Lights out! Put out those lights! Put them out." One grisly episode featured a giant spider that preyed on humans. I still shudder at the

memory of the crunching sound as this loathsome crea-
ture gorged itself on human bones. Radio is a stimulus to
the imagination, conjuring up mental images more com-
pelling, more beautiful, more horrific than the explicit,
contrived images beamed over television.

The advent of television in the fifties was exciting. Our
family had one of the first sets in Montreal, because of a
letter that I wrote. The small local grocery store in our
neighbourhood was planning to expand, and it solicited
suggestions from patrons of the existing store concerning
needed improvements. The suggestions I made included
concentrating the canned goods in one place, instead of
scattering them throughout the store; disposing of the
large, empty cartons that cluttered the aisles; and relocat-
ing the open, hazardous stairway situated in the middle
of the store and leading to the basement. To my surprise
and delight, I won the contest. Incidentally, I don't know
if there were any other entrants. The prize was a large,
handsome Stromberg-Carlson combination television and
radio. Our family was very excited about this development, especially since the coronation of Queen Elizabeth
II on June 2, 1953, was fast approaching. We invited some
friends to witness the event on this new marvel. We were
all fascinated and moved by the sight of the young queen,
looking lonely and vulnerable in her simple white gown,
as she took the oath and was anointed and crowned by
the Archbishop of Canterbury.

Our entertainment did not include movies, because,
in Quebec at that time, no one under the age of sixteen
was admitted. This ordinance followed a theatre fire in
which more than 70 children were trampled to death try-
ing to escape. Many bodies were piled up beside doors
that opened inward. After this tragedy, another ordinance required that the doors to all public buildings

open outward.

Other recreational activities were limited. On the street, girls skipped rope, played hopscotch, or just sat on the curbs and talked. I still marvel at the appearance of chalk or some substitute when we needed it to draw our hopscotch diagrams on the pavement. They seemed to come out of nowhere. When chalk did not appear, we made do with a piece of glass with which to scratch out our diagrams. Unless it rained, the diagrams lasted for some time. In those days, we played freely on the pavements, since there were few cars in our working-class neighbourhood. The boys played baseball in empty lots, swinging homemade bats and using large pieces of cardboard as bases. I also remember that boys congregated in small groups on street corners, talking as they jiggled from one foot to another, hands in pockets, and calling out to passing girls. Sometimes we went walking in the nearby woods, which were all built over in subsequent years. A favourite pastime of my friend Kitty Lang and me was the two-mile walk in the blistering summer sun to Woolworth's, where we consumed five-cent ice cream sodas. That was a big afternoon! In the winter, some of us would walk a few miles through the snow, braving the bitter wind, to a small kiosk where we could buy hot chocolate for a nickel. After consuming the hot chocolate, we were still cold, because we wore long woollen coats that were no match for the cold winds and freezing temperatures. There was nothing like the wind and waterproof jackets that keep us warm today.

I have said that the winters were harsh, but, on the other hand, it is hard not to wax lyrical about the beauty of a fine winter day, with its crisp air, the sun shining from an azure sky, and a fresh fall of snow crunching underfoot. The pristine snow brings a special kind of quiet to the world. The ordinary sounds of life are muffled, and a hush creeps over the landscape. My mother especially loved still winter evenings, when the stars came out and a cold, bright moon illumined the whitened landscape. It cast its spell over the tree outside our dining room window, tracing its thin, bare branches on the glistening snow in black, delicate, yet distinct outline. "Come here," my mother commanded, adding, "you have to see this. It reminds me of Robert Frost's poem, 'Stopping by Woods on a Snowy Evening.'"

Few Depression kids owned skates, skis, or toboggans, and so it fell to us to find such winter diversions as we could. We pelted each other with snowballs, reared tall snow forts, and created fat snowmen who had black coals for eyes and who sported jaunty red toques atop their heads.

A favourite diversion of mine, when I was a kid, involved finding a long, slick ribbon of black ice, which appeared like magic in the snow. I would stand back about a hundred yards in the snow, begin to run, and, gathering momentum, hit the ice to sail fearlessly along the path, arms outstretched like an errant bird, at a giddy speed until I stumbled into the waiting snow at the end of the path.

Among the few planned activities was the winter sleigh ride. About a dozen of us high school kids piled into the open sleigh under a serene night sky lit by starry gems. We sang popular songs, gossiped, argued, exchanged friendly insults, told jokes, flirted, and jostled each other. In the meantime, the sleigh glided gracefully between the glistening snowbanks to the rhythmic, muffled beat of the horse's hooves as he patiently traversed the terrain. After the sleigh ride, the crowd, rosy-cheeked from the frosty air and high in spirit, came to our home.

They climbed the two flights of stairs to our third-floor flat and crammed themselves good-naturedly into the small rooms. There my mother, always tolerant and generous in spirit, served them hot chocolate and homemade cookies.

As the seasons changed, we still delighted in outdoor activities. There were few playgrounds, and most of them contained some slides and a miniscule pool. In the summer, it was too hot to visit the playgrounds. Some of our best times, as children, were our forays into the surrounding woods and meadows now covered, alas, with houses, apartments, and condominiums. There we gathered colourful paintbrushes, white Queen Anne's lace, buttercups, wild daisies, and blue cornflowers. The latter grew in profusion on the steep banks of a nearby aqueduct, whose waters sparkled in the afternoon sunlight. In the fall, Tom gathered bittersweet from a source that he refused to reveal to me, perhaps because the bright orange berries endeared him to my mother, and he didn't wish to share the praise with me. Sometimes, on the weekend, my father would take us on walks to a park that nestled beside the aqueduct. With its flaming maple trees and golden oak, the park was beautiful in the fall, and we took pleasure in scuffing through the fallen leaves. Always, my father had a pocket filled with biscuits that he shared with us. How simple were our pleasures!

# Chapter 2

SO UNHAPPY were my schooldays that I am reluctant to write about them. I began in Grade 1 at age five (there were few kindergartens in those days) in a four-room school not far from my home. I vividly recall this scene of my humiliation. The art assignment was to produce a drawing or a painting of a banana. Evidently my rendition of this fruit was so offensive that the teacher held it up to ridicule by the whole class. Moreover, she summoned Tom from the next room, Grade 2, to view this disaster. I was not the only victim of this cruel teacher. I learned that, in her previous Grade 1 class, the best friend of my cousin Alan had peed on the floor in Alan's absence. This teacher made sure that she informed Alan, upon his return to class, about his friend's accident. From then on, I distrusted all teachers, though I had some pleasant ones in the next few years.

A different problem reared its head when I was in Grade 2. It was decided at Christmas that I had mastered the requirements of Grade 2, and I was transferred for the second term to Grade 3, where I joined my eight-year-old brother. I didn't learn, until years later, of his extreme discomfiture at this unexpected development. As for me, uprooted and separated from my friends, I became so ill that it was decided to return me to Grade 2 to finish out the term.

When I arrived eventually in Grade 5 I encountered yet another teacher who was harsh in voice and manner. I was so terrified of her that I worked hard in order to avoid censure, with the result that I scored 98.5% in that grade. The situation was made more miserable by the fact that I developed a pronounced stutter. Instead of letting me alone, the teacher called on me. I would stand up and begin to stutter, feeling a hot red tide creeping up my neck and into my face, as titters spread throughout the classroom. Many years later, I encountered this ogre again, who exclaimed, "I will always remember your record in Grade 5." I didn't tell her the reason for that record.

It is no wonder that I hated school with a passion. Every August I became morose as I contemplated returning to school in the following month. It must be remembered that, in those days, teachers reigned supreme in their classrooms and that parents had little or no say in what went on. They were, indeed, kept at arm's length. Thus, there were no consultations between teachers and parents and no parent-teacher associations, as there are today. I never complained to my parents, because we lived then in an age of authority, and my parents would see themselves and the teachers as authority figures. Thus they lent each other tacit support. If we got in trouble at school, worse trouble awaited us at home.

A prime symbol of this age of authority was the omnipresent strap, a hard leather object about eight inches in length by three inches in width. When some unfortunate child was about to receive the strap, the principal, who administered it, opened wide the doors of all the classrooms on that floor, as a warning to potential malefactors. I still remember how I shivered and shook when I heard the resounding slap of that hard leather strap on the small hands of the hapless victims. Today this practice would be labelled "child abuse." One could argue that it produced a kind of terrified respect for authority that kept kids in line. It could be argued that genuine respect is never attained by such harsh means. This example is a small illustration of how the age of authority produced a high degree of stability and order in society that is unlikely to be seen again.

Where children were concerned, in the 1930s, 1940s and through the 1950s, the Victorian dictum that children were to be seen and not heard still held sway. Everyone knew his or her proper place, especially children. A friend of mine gave me a small illustration from her personal experience. When her parents issued a command that seemed unreasonable to her and she protested, she was told "Don't talk back!" She remarked to me, "It wasn't fair, because I often had a valid point that I wasn't allowed to express." I have sometimes reflected that we children didn't know our own power, and our parents and teachers were wise enough to keep that knowledge from us. Today psychologists, counsellors, and others have, to a great extent, unleashed this power.

I recall a situation from my fourth grade class that haunts me still. There was a little mixed-race boy named Robert Waters. I remember chiefly the glow that was always about him. His big brown eyes shone, his hair shone, and the skin of his face shone. He was always impeccably dressed. I am ashamed to say that no one among us ever spoke to him, nor did the teacher address him. I have asked myself since whether we were racist or whether it was simply that he was different, and we didn't know how to deal with him. I fault the teacher, who could have used the opportunity to teach us tolerance, and even love, for people who were different from us. But she didn't. Robert came and went in silence. I think that he must have been the loneliest little boy in the world.

High school was to produce yet another distressing situation. At that time, there was a so-called "Latin class" which contained the bright students, and there was a "commercial class," which was supposed to prepare children in bookkeeping, shorthand, and typing. I was placed in the commercial class which was actually the dumping ground for those considered unfit to enter the Latin class. We were considered the dregs, and we became known as the "dum-dum class." It contained every level from mentally challenged to intelligent pupils. The reason for my presence in that class was my mother's conviction that it would be well for me to acquire commercial skills so that I could secure a safe position in the Bank of Montreal, as she herself had done. It must be remembered that the only occupations open to women at that time were teacher, nurse, or secretary. It was unheard of for women to aspire to become engineers, lawyers, doctors, or CEOs. To someone like me, who longed to delve deeply into literature and history in particular, the four years were difficult. But I was obedient, as children were in those days, and I suffered through the commercial course. In the process, I did learn skills, notably shorthand and typing, that were to serve me well in succeeding years, and I made some good friends. They were the saving grace of my high school days. Also, wonder of wonders, I captured the history prize in Grade 11, something unknown for a pupil in the dum-dum class. The prize was a book by Lin Yutang entitled My Country and My People, an account of life in China at the time.

Tom, meanwhile, was considered by our parents to be

very clever, a near-genius, and was enrolled in the Latin class. This reinforced my sense of my own mediocrity, but I accepted this verdict and, in fact, admired Tom enormously. Indeed, when I was young, I came close to worshipping him. He was bookish, not much interested in sports except to play the occasional game of golf. I should add that there was tacit disapproval in our family of sports on the grounds that they were anti-intellectual. The attitude was that only people who couldn't do anything else engaged in sports. My sense of inferiority was magnified when he was studying, and we all tiptoed around the flat, lest we disturb him. When he preferred the picture on my scribbler to the one adorning his scribbler, I was forced to give mine up. I felt resentful, but I deferred to him because I felt inferior, unworthy, partly because my school experiences had left me bruised and uncertain. I was to wrestle with this demon for the rest of my life. It was not until I reached early middle age that I discovered that I was as smart as Tom.

The night of my high school graduation was marred for me by the sudden appearance of my good friend Kitty, who had failed Grade 11. As I came down from the platform in my demure long white dress, carrying a bouquet of red roses, I came face to face with her. I was shocked and disbelieving that she would come to the ceremony. We looked at each other, and, next thing I knew, we were weeping in a close embrace. Later, she took a course as a baby nurse, because it didn't require a high school diploma. She was hired by the American wife of a high official in India to care for their baby. The journey to India took six weeks by boat and train. There were no planes in those days. As World War II began, Kitty met and married a British army officer, and they moved to England. We lost touch during the war, and found each other again when they returned to Canada.

I cannot leave this discussion of my high school days without mention of the physical education classes, which I dreaded. They were presided over by a female martinet who put us through our paces by shouting commands and ridiculing anyone who didn't come up to her standard. To begin with, she lined up the class from the shortest girl (about 4 feet, 5 inches) to the tallest, who happened to be my friend Kitty, who topped six feet, an almost unheard-of height for a girl in those days. At five feet nine inches, I was the second tallest girl in the class. This arrangement resulted in the shortest and tallest of us feeling like freaks. Moreover, I was awkward and self-conscious. What agony it was for me to jump on the springboard, from which one was expected to soar gracefully onto a contraption called a "horse," and to do a double-flip atop the horse, with the result that one faced the other way! I managed the springboard, but, instead of executing a graceful reverse flip, I found myself in an ungainly heap on the horse. By this time, the whole class, with the exception of Kitty and myself, had been through the routine, and they lined up, flushed with triumph, to watch us and to laugh at our performance. Kitty did even worse than I did and was also the subject of much mirth. So desperate was I to escape this humiliation that I wrote notes, excusing myself on various grounds and signed my mother's name. I was terrified that she would find out. She would surely kill me, I thought, but that was preferable to resuming gym classes. To my amazement, no one found out the truth.

My informal education was much more enjoyable. My mother read poetry to me from the time I could understand anything about language. She could quote long passages from literature, like Mark Antony's speech over

Caesar's body or Tennyson's long poem "Ulysses." When she scolded me for some transgression, I could always reduce her to helpless laughter by quoting Macbeth's startled comment upon seeing the ghost of the murdered Banquo: "Never shake thy gory locks at me!" She was never without a quotation. When a male friend of ours suffered a disastrous marriage from which he never recovered, she quoted from Othello, "He loved not wisely, but too well." I remember her quoting the poet Robinson's words, when I expressed regret over some incident, "Familiar as an old mistake and futile as regret."

My mother has been gone for more than twenty years, but I am still astounded that I never thought to ask her where she acquired her love of poetry. Did it come from an inspired teacher? From a fellow student? Or did she pick it up on her own, responding instinctively to its language of rhythms and cadences? In an era when many people received only a Grade 8 education, my mother graduated from high school. In fact, she was the only member of her graduating class of 1915. In effect, she was the class. My father, on the other hand, had only a Grade 8 education.

Another feature of my informal education stemmed from my relationship with my maternal grandfather, William Arthur Staines. He and my grandmother lived in a small brick bungalow near our cold-water flat during part of my childhood, and he maintained a big garden. I can still see the rows of cabbages. They would have produced a mountain of coleslaw. There were rows of prickly raspberry bushes, and apple trees that bore lavish pink blossoms in the spring and produced yellow transparent apples in the summer. He had little time for or interest in flowers, but he did grow tall, stately gladioli in vibrant shades of peach, purple, red and white. To this day, I never see gladioli without a pang of recognition. I had my own bean patch in his garden, and I was elated to see the stems pushing their way through the soil toward the light, eventually to produce beans.

I was the favoured grandchild, the only girl among his many grandchildren. For instance, as my mother told me, I was always served a cup of the first peas from the garden, while she and my aunts looked on with envy. My mother also told me that I won his heart when I was still an infant in a crib. Evidently my arms and legs pumped wildly as he approached, an invitation to be picked up that he found irresistible. He was a religious man who conveyed to me his deep faith in God and his love of the Bible. I also gained from him a love of fantasy. One day, when I visited him, he chided me for leaving my three dolls outside on the verandah that extended along the front of the house. "I heard them crying," he said, "and I brought them in." Sure enough, there they were, lying on a couch and covered with a blanket. I felt terrible. Small wonder that today it wouldn't surprise me if my stuffed Paddington bear began to sing or if it were discovered that, after all, the moon really is made of green cheese.

Sometimes I would meet my grandfather on the street. People must have been bemused by the sight of a dignified old gentleman in a straw boater hat striding purposefully along the sidewalk and suddenly ducking behind a tree when he saw his small granddaughter approaching. Just as I came abreast of him, he would pop out, causing me to emit squeals of delight. I never knew another adult who could enter so easily into a child's world.

About this time, I composed a paragraph that described the growth of a tulip bulb that was planted in a small pot. I distinctly remember the thrill I experienced when the first tender, timid shoot penetrated the hard earth—"the force through which the green fuse drives the flower," to quote Dylan Thomas's wonderful metaphor. I recall writing about the slow thickening of the shoot, as it grew steadily and branched out to produce a tiny flower. Nurtured by light and water, the blossom responded by becoming a full-blown tulip, lifting its face to greet the new-found sun. This, then, was the little paragraph that I wrote at age six. My delighted grandfather sent it to one of his numerous sisters in England, and that was the end of that. Unfortunately, in those days, there were no copy machines that would preserve a piece of writing forever. I have often felt curiosity about that little paragraph, wondering how this early piece of writing was put together.

After that initial attempt, I sometimes thought, not very seriously, about becoming a writer. But I could not see writing about my drab world. I had it in my head that writers told stories of glamorous people doing exciting things. I didn't realize that my little working-class world was a rich resource for a writer. People struggled to find jobs that would enable them to support their families, men rode the rails from city to city looking for work, and women scrubbed, scrimped, and took jobs as cleaners in order to support their children. As often happens in times of adversity, people helped each other. They shared their scanty stores of food and they babysat for each other. The poor gathered warm clothing in the winter for their poorer neighbours. I remember that, despite our own hardships, my mother gave a pair of my brother's snow boots, somewhat reluctantly, to a young child who had no protection against the freezing Montreal winter. He was called "Puss," and he passed away near the end of that winter.

I always enjoyed composition classes in school, and I

did well in them. On one occasion, the parents of a female friend asked me to help her with her writing. I had no idea how to proceed. With a combination of her new-found motivation and my clumsy attempts to teach her how to write, her grades improved measurably. Also, in high school, I was asked to write a weekly column in a newspaper, now long defunct, called the "Standard." I contributed to a page that detailed the various activities of high schools across Montreal. I was rewarded with a small payment and my picture in the "Standard." I dimly realized that I might be a promising writer, but I did not pursue the matter. If I could do my time over, I think I might have aspired to become a journalist.

One sidelight of my efforts at writing was the delight I took in writing my name backwards. The result was that "Muriel Tomkins" became "Leirum Snikmot," and I laughed aloud at the absurdity this change had wrought. It was straight out of Lewis Carroll, with his "slithy toves" and "momme raths."

If there was a constant in my childhood, it was the weekly tea party held at my grandparents' house. It was a strictly female affair, hosted by my grandmother and attended by my mother, her two sisters, and me. In the dining room, a large Tiffany-style lamp with beaded fringe hung from the ceiling, casting a pool of light on the shiny, round mahogany table, leaving the rest of the room in gloom. The table was set with a lace cloth, and featured thin cucumber sandwiches, little cakes, jelly rolls, ham, cheese, and, sometimes, English trifle. My presence was tolerated, on the unspoken understanding that I would be quiet. It was still an age when children were to be seen and not heard. Tea was always served promptly at four o'clock, and, to this day, I find myself putting the kettle on at that hour. It is unfortunate that the leisurely, civilized custom of afternoon tea has eroded in the frenzied course of modern life. When I visited England in the 1980s, I looked in vain for the little tea shops that had clustered around the streets of Westminster on my previous visit. Alas, the tea shops had been replaced by pizza parlours and other fast food outlets.

My grandfather died when I was eleven, the first death that I experienced. Like most children, I expected my world to go on forever without changing. It was a hot July afternoon when I last saw him. I noticed that his face and neck were a bright red, partly from the sun and partly from his exertions in cutting back the raspberry canes. I sat on his knee, as usual, and, for the first time, he remarked that I couldn't do so much longer as I was getting too big. How that remark saddened me! For many days after his death, I visited his home, certain that he must be there. Obviously, I was in full denial.

Another aspect of my informal education was that I learned to play the piano. I marvel at the sacrifice my parents must have made to purchase a piano and to enrol us in music lessons. To this day, I don't know how they scraped together the money needed to buy the piano. It reflected their earnest desire to give us whatever cultural advantages they could. It was a handsome upright piano made of oak, and it is still in our family today. I never enjoyed the lessons, and I hated the practice, with the result that my parents stopped my lessons after two years. By that time, I had learned to play the "Blue Danube" waltz rather well, because I liked its sprightly rhythm. Tom also took piano lessons, and he excelled. However, if he liked a tune, he would play it over and over. Such was the case with "I've Got My Love to Keep Me Warm." It's a wonder that our long-suffering neighbours didn't complain.

I remember two experiences that accompanied my

learning to play the piano. One was the experience of visiting my music teacher, a thin, pale little man who always wore a jacket that had once been black, but was turning green with age. He lived with his invalid wife, for whom he was the caregiver, in a dingy, cold-water flat like ours. I'm sure that his piano teaching gave him only a miserly living. The other experience concerned the girl pupil whose lesson preceded mine. I used to sit watching her and waiting, and hating her because she had wonderful long red hair, cascading below her shoulders in the corkscrew ringlets that were popular at the time. By contrast, I had wispy straight nondescript brown hair.

Before my grandfather died, I did derive pleasure from playing the piano while he sang. Sometimes he sang a hymn, but more often, he sang of men who did heroic deeds. For some unaccountable reason, I remember a song about a "little midship mite" who saved the boat from capture by the Russians, as the song went. My grandfather was very earnest about his singing. He would strike a pose, throw his shoulders back, stroke his white hair, hold up his hands as though he were conducting an orchestra, and bellow the words.

Tom and I were bookish children. I remember that, at Christmas, there were many books scattered around the tree, including the Bobbsey Twins series, the Hardy Boys series, and, earlier, the Burgess Bedtime Stories featuring Farmer Brown's boy. Also, I remember my parents attaching candles in holders to the Christmas tree branches and lighting the candles before our wondering eyes for only ten minutes, for fear of causing a fire. There were ornaments and tinsel, but no tree lights in those days. Each year, my father unfailingly exclaimed, "That's the prettiest tree we ever had!" Again, my parents must have made considerable sacrifices to see that our Christmases were merry. My mother would make small bags of white cheesecloth, with red cord drawstrings, and fill them with candy, so that we would have something to share with our friends when they dropped by. Christmas dinner was always postponed for almost a week because my father worked many hours of overtime at the post office to make more money for us. Turkey was a great treat, because it was available only at Christmas. To this day, turkey still has the aura of a treat for me.

In the era in which I grew up, as an English Protestant child in a province that was overwhelmingly French and Catholic, the Catholic church was very powerful. How I longed to be a Catholic! My best friend, Dora Cunnington, was Catholic, and I sometimes attended Mass with her. I was entranced by the crucifix on which the full body of a sad-faced Jesus was displayed. The crucifix held the central place in the church, high above the main altar. The statue of Mary, the mother of Jesus, mesmerized me. There she stood on a platform that was close to the congregation. She was draped in a celestial blue robe in loose folds that shimmered in the light of the dozen or more flickering votive candles. Then came the priest, swinging a censer of incense that filled the church with its overpowering fragrance.

Usually, the highlight of my summer was the annual parade in honour of St. Jean-Baptiste (John the Baptist), patron saint of Quebec. For this major festival, houses along a specified route transformed themselves into church altars. The exterior of the house was completely covered in white or cream satin cloth, yards and yards of it falling from high beams and draped carefully on every side. The idea was that the parade would stop at each house, and the priest would give his blessing at the altar. The procession that stopped at the various houses was impressive. It consisted not only of the priest and other church officials wearing elaborate robes, but rows and rows of little girls. Clad in their First Communion white lacy dresses, with bridal headdresses and wearing long white stockings, they walked solemnly through the streets, eyes downcast and chanting what I presumed was the catechism. A huge crowd always followed the procession through the local streets. I joined the crowd one hot summer evening. I was transfixed, kneeling with all the rest when the priest raised the host. So absorbed was I in this ritual that I didn't notice the time and didn't realize that dense darkness had fallen, relieved only by the flickering street lights. Finally, I abandoned the procession and went home to find my parents beside themselves with worry. At the time, I was puzzled as to why my parents shook me violently. If they were so happy to see me, why this rather rough treatment? Of course, I understood much later that a strong sense of relief sometimes breeds strange behaviour.

My parents disapproved mightily of my fascination with Catholicism, for they thought of it as an oppressive religion. Rumours flew, in the English Protestant community, that priests went to people's houses to tell them how to vote or to raise questions with couples who had been married for nine months and hadn't produced a child. Also, there was speculation that each Catholic family with more than four children was expected to give one child to the church to become a priest or a nun. I don't know whether there was any truth to those rumours, but they were pervasive.

I grew up with many Catholic children in a French-speaking neighbourhood. Thus, my earliest playmates were French kids with whom I had agreeable relationships, and I picked up a kind of street French. Then, when I began to attend English schools, I left some of my French playmates behind.

I have always been proud of the concord that existed between the English and French in my native Quebec, considering that French Canada was a conquered nation. English and French citizens existed peacefully, side by side, for nearly 300 years, not riven by strife and violence, as so often happens in cultures that consist of groups with different languages, different religions, and different customs and values. To be sure, Quebec came close to separating from Canada on several occasions. Perhaps the most volatile event was the strident call by French President Charles de Gaulle, when he visited Quebec in the 1960s. "Vive le Québec libre!" he shouted from the balcony of the Montreal City Hall. It was a tense moment in the country's history, but the traditionally temperate Canadian nature soon prevailed.

I remember only one hostile occasion. I was on my way to school with my English friends when we encountered a band of French kids going in the opposite direction to their school. We threw stones at each other, not out of hate, because I don't recall feeling hate, but simply, I suppose, because they were different from us, and each side felt compelled to throw stones. Fortunately, none of the stones reached their destination, which suggests that neither side was ready to do battle!

I loved the sound of church bells emanating from the many Catholic churches in our neighbourhood. Peals rang out on Sunday morning all over the city, as the faithful flocked to Mass. To this day, my ears perk up when I hear church bells. There were huge convents and monasteries in the city. As a young girl, my mother attended piano classes at one of the convents. Evidently, a nun would sit in the center of the room while young girls practised on the piano. My mother claimed that, with all these girls playing different pieces, the little nun could at once detect a wrong note. I give much credit to the nuns and priests of my youth. They seemed to me to be good people who cared about their charges and were utterly devoted to the church to which they had dedicated their lives. We often think of nuns and priests as cloistered beings who emerge hardly at all from their cells. But, as a matter of fact, many of them do productive work. At Oka, close to Montreal, the monks produced a cheese that became famous, and the nuns on Nun's Island, in the St. Lawrence River close to Verdun, grew products like corn, beans, tomatoes and onions.

Many nuns were teachers or nurses. I used to feel sorry for them during the hot, humid Montreal summers. They were encased in high-necked, long, black habits that almost swept the ground. Their heads were tightly covered in black wimples and their sleeves were long and close-fitting.

If the lives of the nuns were circumscribed by their clothing and the strict rules of their orders, other women suffered from more subtle forms of control. The roles of the sexes were sharply differentiated. Women were expected to be sweet, decorative, virginal, and compliant with the wishes of men. Men went out to earn a living, while women stayed home to run the household and to bear and raise children almost single-handedly. It was a domestic partnership in which fathers had little to do with the rearing of their children. Indeed, it would have been considered almost unmanly for a husband to change a diaper or cook a meal. Like many others, my father travelled daily across the city by bus and streetcar. Often he waited for hours on street corners, a situation that grew worse in the winter when snow and freezing temperatures caused long delays. Frequently, he also worked on Saturdays, especially at times such as Christmas and Easter, when the mail was heavy. It was a typical daily routine that had a significant effect on family life. Fathers became almost strangers to their children, rarely seen apart from weekends. To Tom and me, our father was a figure who appeared, exhausted, at the dinner table and retired shortly thereafter to recover from the rigours of the day.

Many women sought marriage unthinkingly because, despite its narrow limits, it secured for them instant and enduring social approval. Few women worked outside the home and career choices were extremely limited. Basically, women could become teachers, nurses, secretaries, or clerks. There were few women lawyers, engineers, accountants, or doctors. When I was growing up in Montreal, there was one woman doctor, and she was considered something of an oddity. I bought into these concepts, which circumscribed the opportunities for both men and women, because I didn't know any better. At the same time, something in me rebelled against the limits on women's career aspirations, and the struggle caused me some confusion. As a result, I developed a distrust of men.

World War II was to cause a dramatic shift in the entrenched roles of men and women. As the men volunteered or were drafted for military service, women poured into the factories, offices, and shops to fill the vacant positions. "Rosie the Riveter" became the poster child, the symbol of this new breed of women.

I turn now to a discussion of some moral standards of my generation. To members of the present generation, living, as they do, in a society suffused with sex in all its aspects, our standards must seem as strange as the annals of a forgotten civilization. Premarital sex was almost unheard of and roundly condemned. So was homosexuality, which was kept well hidden. Those who practiced premarital sex brought disgrace upon themselves and their families. This hush-hush attitude had a restraining effect on young girls, though it must be admitted that fear of pregnancy (in the absence of modern contraceptives) kept them in line. If premarital sex was condemned, pregnancy outside of marriage was even more harshly censured. A friend put it this way: "If I had become pregnant while unmarried, my parents would have disowned me." I knew of only one instance where a schoolmate of mine was suspected of becoming pregnant. She suddenly disappeared, returning some months later, considerably slimmer, to resume life as though nothing had happened. In those cases, the babies were discreetly put up for adoption, or else they were absorbed into the family as if the girl's parents had produced a child. Around this time, my friends and I got hold of a book about a nun who had a baby, and we were both shocked and titillated.

Of course, the girls, like Hester Prynne in <u>The Scarlet Letter</u>, were condemned, but not the boys. Society turned a blind eye to their participation, even as it tolerated the idea that some young men must "sow their wild oats."

Although I cannot prove it, I will claim that nearly all the young girls of my age, including me, were virgins when they married. This condition was partly the result of strict societal control, and there were economic reasons, too. Most of us could not afford to have our own apartments, and we lived at home under our parents' watchful eyes. A few of my friends whose parents did not live in Montreal rented a single room, often with a shared bath, in someone else's apartment or house.

In those days, the mention of sex was taboo. My

mother would never talk about sex, and it was left to me to find out for myself such mysteries as menstruation, intercourse, and pregnancy. I heard about intercourse when I was fourteen from my good friend Kitty, who said matter-of-factly, "He puts his thing inside of you." I was shocked. It sounded like a violation to me, and I decided not to think about it. Kitty also told me about menstruation. I reacted with disbelief and immediately consulted my mother, who reluctantly conceded that it did exist. That was the beginning and end of my discussion of sex with her. I know now that she came from a generation of women who were fearful concerning sex. Some regarded it as an inexplicable male compulsion forced on women. It is small wonder, then, that all of these factors produced negative feelings and fear, if not an aversion to sex.

Another feature of the society in which I grew up was its unspoken commitment to protecting its helpless citizens, old people and children. For example, old people lived with their families. A cousin of mine claimed that she could never remember a time when an elderly relative was not living in her home. Today, many older people are shuffled off to retirement homes or nursing homes. These places have proliferated over the past thirty years.

As for children, I am sure that child abuse existed, but I have no idea of its extent, since the subject, like the subject of sex, was not mentioned. A jolting experience that I had at the age of twelve offers an example of this attitude. I came out of school one day to find our landlord waiting in his car to give me a lift home. He lived in the first-floor flat of our building, and we lived in the third-floor flat. I thought it was nice of him to drive me home, but I was surprised when, instead of dropping me in front of our building, he drove straight into the garage. He stopped, turned off the ignition, and said, "I think you have something to show me." I wasn't sure what he meant, but the glint in his gimlet eyes and the tone of his voice frightened me. I scrambled out of the car, rushed through the garage, panted along the sidewalk, and raced up the two flights of stairs to our flat. From then on, I stayed out of his way. I decided not to tell my parents, partly because of the reticence bred in me, partly because I was afraid my father would fly into one of his rages and perhaps kill our landlord. At the very least, my parents would want to move, and I dreaded the upheaval. Since that encounter, I have wondered how many abused children fail, for a variety of reasons, to report such incidents to their parents.

I also kept from my parents that Kitty and I tried our hand at smoking. The experiment began one day when an unthinking uncle left an open pack of cigarettes on Kitty's kitchen table. We filched a couple of cigarettes, found a secluded spot underneath the stairs, and lit up. We felt very daring and not a little guilty. I don't think that either of us enjoyed the experience, but neither of us was about to admit it. After all, in the very act, weren't we showing that we were grown up, sophisticated!

Undoubtedly, the moral standards of my generation were harsh and restrictive in many ways, but they produced a high degree of stability and order, stemming from the rigid code that established black and white lines. One course of action was right, one was wrong, and there was little middle ground. The breakdown in order really began with World War I, when many crowned heads of Europe met their doom. The most notable happening was, of course, the overthrow of the 300-year old Romanov dynasty in Russia, where the Tsar had long been revered as a God-appointed ruler. The Depression and World War II were further unsettling factors and the changes reached a crescendo in the 1950s. My discussion is, to be sure, an oversimplification of some events of the twentieth century, in which I spent most of my life. But I have presented them as a backdrop, however inadequate, to explain some of the forces that shaped me.

We were the products of a period of unprecedented global economic and political turmoil, and an educational system that has been rightly criticized for its rote learning, its often harsh methods, and its scant attention to the real needs and interests of children. But perhaps, after all, we owe something to those circumstances, for, on the whole, we turned out to be a disciplined, responsible generation. Tom Brokaw has labelled us "the greatest generation" in his book of the same name, because of the trials we endured and because of our accomplishments in rebuilding our own economy and restoring the shattered nations of Europe after World War II. Also, I'm glad that I grew up in the quiet, safe world of my childhood and youth, an environment that, sadly, we may never experience again.

# Chapter 3

AFTER GRADUATION from high school, Tom and I went to work in separate banks. College was out of the question. I remember the sad expression on my father's face when he said to us, as we were finishing high school, "I can only give you high school. I can't give you college." We replied, "That's all right. We'll manage." We exhibited a bravado that we did not really feel.

I entered the Bank of Montreal in 1938 at the age of sixteen, fresh out of high school. The bank, founded in 1817 and still located on St. James Street in Montreal's financial district, was an imposing stone structure, embodying the spirit of Victorian stability, order, and supreme confidence. The outside of the building was dominated by four massive stone columns. Inside this august institution, huge, gleaming marble columns soared skyward from the marble floors toward a majestic dome that flooded the rotunda with light. People talked in low voices, and the atmosphere was hushed, as though the rotunda were in awe of itself.

Amid all this splendour, I felt dwarfed and intimidated. After wandering through a maze of halls, I found the typing pool that was to be my workplace for the next two years. It was a huge room with high arched windows and it contained no fewer than twenty desks, arranged in rows and equipped with typewriters. The stern-faced woman, white-haired with the beginnings of a grey mustache, occupied a platform with her assistant from which they could survey their young charges. The result was a prison-like atmosphere, and the din and clatter of the typewriters was deafening.

I was a junior stenographer. The only lower position was that of a uniformed messenger boy, who occupied a tall stool facing a wall-type desk until he was summoned to take papers from one place to another. The bank was paternalistic. It provided a free lunch every day in a gloomy basement dining room lit by artificial light. Also, medical care was free, and so were the modest pensions which employees received after thirty years. I spent my days carrying around what was known as a stenographer's notebook and two sharpened pencils. In the book I inscribed in shorthand the memoranda and letters dictated by men who, I later realized, were destined never to reach the middle range, let alone the upper echelons of prestige and power. I was expected to transcribe my notes exactly as they were dictated. No initiative was required. In fact, it was discouraged.

I earned $45.00 per month, half of which I gave to my parents for room and board. This salary was miniscule, to be sure, but it must be remembered that one could buy a pair of leather shoes or a handbag for $1.98. Once I coveted a beautiful blue felt hat that cost $5.00, but it was out of my reach. In those days, no self-respecting woman would go to work without wearing a hat and gloves. In the large department stores, millinery departments stretched as far as the eye could see. Today you are lucky to find a few hats mounted on a rack. Also, women always wore dresses. Usually there was a "best dress" reserved for Sunday wear. Pants were a no-no, except for picnics and sports events. My mother was happy that her daughter was working in a safe, secure, benevolent environment. At the end of two years, I was assigned to a department where I worked for two or three men. A few years later, I was finally appointed as secretary to a department manager. It was a small step upward, but I felt relieved that, at last, I had a certain status, and it was good to get away from the din and clatter of the crowded typing pool.

In 1939, when I was 17, World War II erupted. The war had little effect on our daily lives. Rationing was not severe, the conflict in Europe seemed remote, and we weren't bombed or invaded. To me, the greatest impact of the war was the heartbreaking loss of a number of the boys in my classes. They included Charlie Barton, the dentist's son; Don Peterson and Fred King, who were best friends; Victor Ashton, an only child whose father had been killed in World War I; and the identical Forster twins, who enjoyed confusing people because of the strong resemblance between them. There was little of the idealism that had characterized World War I. Rather, the attitude, at least among my contemporaries, was that Hitler had to be stopped in his monstrous course. It was a dirty job, and the sooner it was over with, the better. It must be admitted, however, that there were young men and women who welcomed war as a taste of high adventure. We were all fired up by Churchill's soaring rhetoric and the example set by the King and Queen of England in refusing to leave London and touring areas that had been hard hit by German bombers.

On the other hand, I had always known that my mother was a rabid pacifist, an attitude born of her perceptions of World War I and its aftermath. High idealism had given way to cynicism as casualties mounted, the war turned into a slaughter, and veterans coming home faced a bleak future. "No war is worth fighting," she declared, vigorously and often, her big brown eyes flashing. Because of her anti-war, anti-military stance, she wouldn't allow Tom or me to join the Boy Scouts and Girl Guides, on the grounds that these were quasi-military organizations. Actually, the only military overtones could be found in the uniforms and periodic parades. I used to watch with envy as my friends went off to Brownie pack meetings, toasted marshmallows around campfires, sang patriotic songs, and marched in parades carrying Canadian flags. Inevitably, my mother's attitude rubbed off on Tom and me, so that we didn't enlist in the war. I later regretted that we had failed to do our part.

If World War II was a tragedy that engulfed millions of people, it benefited some. I am thinking, in particular, of two boys who were constantly turning up at our home during my high school years. Russell Charters and Walter Macdonald came, like Tom and me, from working-class families, where there was no money for a college education. They almost always appeared on Sunday evenings, when my mother would bake wonderful chocolate cake, lemon tarts, and other treats. These boys were very different. Russell was stable, serious. Walter was mercurial, fun-loving. I believe that I could have married either of these boys, partly as the result of propinquity, partly because young men going off to war seem to want to marry and produce a child as if to secure a kind of immortality.

However, I wasn't interested, as I had two great desires. I decided that I would make my life as interesting, even exciting, as possible. I would travel, and I would get a great education. At that time, the possibility of realising this dream was almost laughable, as remote as the stars in the midnight sky. But I clung to the hope, nevertheless. I believe that my desire for travel was prompted partly by reading about the great British heroes whose exploits were glorified in our history books. They included Clive of India, Lord Nelson, and the Duke of Wellington. My desire to travel was also inspired as the direct result of attending a lecture given by a young woman who had actually visited India. It must be remembered that people travelled very little in those days. I don't recall what she said, only that I was fascinated by being in her presence, and I wanted just to touch her because she had been to that far-off exotic land.

Walter and Russell returned unscathed from their war-time experiences as pilots in the Royal Canadian Air Force. A grateful nation rewarded them with the opportunity to attend college at government expense. They completed college and launched forth into highly successful careers. Eventually, Walter's passion for flying, which began in high school and was fulfilled during his service in World War II, led him to an important government position in aviation. Russell, who became a mining engineer, advanced to the presidency of a large mining company. Had the war not come along, they would never have enjoyed these opportunities.

An unexpected outcome of the war, as far as I was concerned, was the breaking up of some long-term friendships. I have in mind two close friends, Eilleen Smith and Maisie Stone, who, together with Kitty, Alice James, and me, formed a coterie. Eilleen and Maisie were swept off their feet by two Australian airmen, who, like thousands of other Aussies, took flight training in Canada during the war. After the war, Eilleen and Maisie travelled to Australia as war brides, and we never saw them again.

The reason was that air travel between the two countries was rare at that time.

It was during the war (specifically in 1940) that my grandmother, who had survived my grandfather by eight years, died of natural causes—that is, old age. In her will, she left the small brick bungalow that my grandparents had inhabited to my mother. None of us could believe that, at long last, we would live in a house of our own. It was a relief to leave behind the series of cold-water flats and intrusive, sometimes noisy neighbours, and to enjoy the luxury of central heating and hot water tanks. In those days, central heating was provided by a basement furnace fed by masses of coal lodged in a nearby bin, and the ashes had to be disposed of every day. In the kitchen, there was a stove, also fed by coal, featuring several pipes that led to a chimney. Once a year, the pipes had to be dismantled and cleaned. The soot went everywhere. It was a messy job for my parents.

Typically, my mother set out to transform the grounds. She employed a Dutch gardener who replaced the raspberry bushes, the cabbages, and other vegetables with an expanse of lawn. She retained the apple trees, which yielded yellow transparent apples from which she made sparkling, unexpectedly red jelly. The lawn was bordered with flowers, which she attended lovingly. Dahlias, impatiens, petunias, day lilies, and large peonies all grew in colourful profusion. As for the house, it was compact and comfortable. The bungalow had only two bedrooms, so she had another one added. I was delighted with the move. Being of a romantic nature, living in my beloved grandfather's old home was very appealing to me.

# Chapter 4

ICONTINUED TO work in the bank, and I lasted there for seven years. How I ever got up the courage to leave the safety and comfort of that cocoon I'll never know. The impetus came from an advertisement in the local paper, announcing that an international organization was seeking secretaries. It was the International Air Transport Association (IATA), which had existed before the war as an association of European airlines. The year was 1946. IATA was revived, this time as an association of international airlines. Heading up the organization was Sir William Hildred, director general, who liked to be called "D.G." He reported to an executive committee that consisted of airline presidents. The No. 2 man, who hired me as his secretary, was Dr. Henry J. Gorecki. He was a bachelor, a Pole, who had graduated from the University of Cracow and who had headed up the Polish airline, "LOT", before the war. Henry was about 45 years old, short, fat, and balding, with a sharp wit and a sharper eye. Because he had lived with Polish resistance fighters in England during the war, he never mastered the English language. He would begin each explanation with the words, "Eet ees such a situation..." and then he would go on to describe whatever was troubling him. I remember one hilarious occasion when he was talking to some airline personnel about the inadequate funds that had been approved by the executive committee. He complained, "We have to go like buggers to the executive committee." I saw suppressed laughter on several faces, and I managed to contain my own laughter. Afterwards, I told him about his blunder.

Working for IATA was an exciting experience. As a new organization, it was untrammelled by established conventions, protocols, and practices, which become necessary, it seems, as an organization expands. The springtime of an organization closely parallels the springtime of youth, when the world is a fresh new place, vital, and full of promise. There were persons of different nationalities among the IATA employees—British, French, Polish, Czech, Russian, Hungarian, American. Most secretaries were, like me, Canadian. Given the herculean task of repairing the shattered state of civil aviation after the war, there was much coming and going to all the major capitals of the world. I came to know New York, London, and Paris almost as well as I knew Montreal, and, over my seven-year period with IATA, I was sent to many capitals, often with several other secretaries. In these strange new surroundings, we felt no fear because the world was stable and relatively safe. For instance, when I worked in the Paris office of IATA, I frequently finished at 11:00 p.m., locked the office, and walked the half-mile or so back to the hotel. Who would dare to do such a thing today?

We worked hard, taking minutes of meetings of the world airline executives who made up the executive committee, doing various errands for them, and working closely with the staff of the host airline. Often we worked most of the night, preparing position papers, so that next morning the various committees would have a record of the previous day's deliberations. We didn't mind. We were young, full of energy, and captivated by our new surroundings.

I became so adept at gauging Henry's responses that, when a letter arrived, I would draft a reply and send both letters to him. Most of the time, he approved my reply and even praised it. Despite his limited command of English, he had an almost uncanny ability to recognize good expression when he saw it. Henry had three male assistants, who made more than twice my salary of $4,000.00 per year. Henry once confided in me, "If you weren't a woman, I would make you one of my assistants." If the glass ceiling is thick today, it was impenetrable then! I was too young and naive at the time to realise that, quite naturally, his assistants were envious of my knowledge of some important matters that he did not share with them.

We had an interesting relationship in addition to our roles as secretary and boss. We were good friends who understood each other. I discovered, to my surprise, during an incident in Rio de Janeiro, that he had a protective attitude toward me. On one occasion, I had worked hard all day and, when I was invited by a young Brazilian to go dancing at a nightclub called the Vogue, I seized the opportunity. Next morning, Henry asked me what I had done the previous evening. I rarely lie. The moral aspects aside, lying poses risks such as the slow erosion of others' trust in us and the slow loss of the ability to separate truth from falsehood. But, on this occasion, I lied. I told him that I had gone to bed early. "I saw you at the Vogue," he said. I was embarrassed at being caught red-handed, and I replied, "It's none of your business what I do after hours. I don't want any of this 'in loco parentis' stuff." I was touched, chastened, and oddly amused by his reply: "You are a good and decent girl, and I am responsible to your parents." At that point, he had met my parents on several occasions and was much taken by my mother. With her black hair, sparkling brown eyes, and vivacious manner, she reminded him of French women, whose beauty and vivacity he greatly admired.

The rewarding aspect of my new job was, of course, travel. I visited major cities including New York, Rio de Janeiro, Brussels, San Francisco, Nice, Geneva, and Cairo. This most exciting period of my life began in October, 1946, when I was assigned to a month's stay in London, and a month's stay in Cairo. Civil aviation had all but disappeared during the war, and plane travel was a novelty. As I took off from Dorval Airport in Montreal, I noticed that many people had gathered at the airport to watch enviously as I and a few colleagues walked across the tarmac to the plane. There were no jets in those days, only piston aircraft that were, of course, much slower. I remember clearly the excitement that accompanied the announcement that Air France had flown from New York to Paris in seventeen hours. Today the trip would be completed in less than half that time.

Usually IATA people were the only ones on the plane. As a result, we often received one-on-one service from the flight attendants, called "stewardesses" in those days. In London, I attended committee meetings, writing minutes in shorthand and transcribing them later. Whenever I could, I slipped away to see the sights. The city was recovering slowly from the ruin wrought by German bombs during the war in the form of shattered buildings and piles of rubble. But I was heartened by the sight of the storied dome of St. Paul's Cathedral. The dome had survived the fury of German bombs, because of the vigilance of fire wardens, and it rose serenely above the carnage as though in celebration of British courage and endurance. As a long-time history buff, I was thrilled by my visits to Westminster Abbey, especially the Poets' Corner, and the Tower of London, where so many unfortunate persons of high estate had been imprisoned and/or executed on the order of capricious kings and queens. The past melted into the present at Hampton Court Palace, as I imagined I could hear the swish of Anne Boleyn's skirt as she danced with King Henry VIII.

My next stop was Cairo, which presented a totally different culture from anything I had known. This locale was chosen for IATA's first annual general meeting (AGM), at which the executive committee reported to the members and plans would be made for IATA's future development. Each AGM was held at the invitation of a major airline in whatever city it was located. Thus, we traveled to Rio de Janeiro as guests of VARIG, to San Francisco as guests of American Airlines, to Cairo as guests of the Egyptian airline, to Brussels as guests of SABENA, and so on. The airlines vied with each other to provide superb accommodation and entertainment for their guests. They were kind enough to include the lowly secretaries, though we noticed that we were often seated behind the potted palms. I felt as if I were moving in a dream, for I was living in a luxurious style such as I could never have imagined. It was so far from my humble beginnings. I should explain that, in the beginning, IATA hired local secretaries in various cities, but the plan failed as they did not understand the workings and the vocabulary of IATA. It proved easier, and more efficient, to fly the secretaries from Montreal. Often I carried thousands of dollars in American money because that currency was highly valued in Europe at the time. Also, I carried bulky suitcases bursting with documents to be used at the conferences, because there were few, if any, copying facilities available in the cities I visited.

As I write this memoir, the mention of Cairo conjures up perhaps the most vivid memory I have of my IATA experiences. Six of us flew from London in a converted Halifax bomber that was forced to land because the fuel pipe had been lost. The plane landed in the desert outside of Tripoli, where a smallpox epidemic was raging. A large yellow moon hung low in the sky. We found ourselves booked for the night in an old British army barracks that was pockmarked with bullets from the battles fought between British soldiers and the German Afrika Corps under the skilful direction of General Rommel. Whereas the other passengers complained about the inconvenience, I was ecstatic over this brief encounter with history.

Often IATA staff received special treatment. On this occasion, the pilot obligingly flew around the Sphinx and the Pyramids just as the sun was setting in fiery splendour, casting a ruddy glow over the desert. As we circled these ancient ruins, I fancied that the Sphinx followed our progress, turning on us the impassive gaze that had watched the foibles and follies of men across the "lone and level sands" for countless centuries.

In my memory, two other conferences stand out clearly. One was the Geneva meeting, where Swissair had arranged for an elaborate dinner to be held at the Castle of Chillon. We boarded a special train from Geneva to Chillon, disembarked, and found ourselves on a winding gravel path lit by flaring torches, just the dramatic touch I needed to put me in mind of Byron's poem, "The Prisoner of Chillon," though we didn't see any dungeons.

On another occasion, we were guests of American Airlines at a stunning dinner party in the heart of the towering redwood forest, known as Muir Woods, near San

Francisco. The majestic trees are so tall that no sunlight filters to ground level. It is a scene of perpetual twilight. Long tables shone with fine china, crystal, and silver, with flowers and candles at intervals. Singing waiters, resplendent in tuxedos and black tie, moved among the ancient trees, carrying trays laden with food on their shoulders to the delighted guests. To a young person like me, who had lived on the edge of poverty, getting my two pairs of shoes alternately soled and resoled, the event was dazzling.

A third unusual event occurred when I was working at the Hotel Negresco in Nice. One morning, during an early walk on the beach, I encountered a man named Gabriel Dionne, Minister of Tourism for the Principality of Monaco. He offered me a vacation in Monaco, all expenses paid, as a guest of the government. He said that he would send a car for me on a certain date, when the conference would be finished. Since I was a secretary with little influence, I mentally dismissed the offer. But, sure enough, on the appointed day, a chauffeur-driven limousine drew up to the Hotel Negresco, flying the flag of Monaco and bearing the royal crest. I decided to go, and I soon found myself at the Hotel de Paris, the best hotel at that time in the Principality. The window of my room, which was beautifully furnished, looked out to sea. The hotel food was wonderful, as was the service. At breakfast, my half-grapefruit arrived in a small silver bowl embedded in crushed ice that filled a larger silver bowl. Dinner in the magnificent dining room was an occasion, featuring two orchestras, one at each end of the room, that played alternately.

On the dresser in my room was a note from Mr. Dionne's secretary, telling me that she would be coming by in the morning to take me to see the sights of Monaco. As promised, she arrived at the hotel, and we set off for the Jardin Exotique, followed by a visit to the casino. I didn't gamble, but I spent some time studying the patrons gathered around the clicking roulette wheel. One woman, in particular, caught my attention. She was riveted to the spot, never taking her eyes from the roulette wheel as it spun around while the croupier, in black tie, gathered the chips. This happened in the morning, and I couldn't resist returning in the afternoon. It seemed as if the woman hadn't moved from the chair she had occupied in the morning. She was still riveted to the spot. From this incident, I think I understood, in small degree, the grip that gambling exerts over some people.

I remained at the hotel for three days, aware that I had to return to Nice to pack up IATA documents and my belongings. I never saw Mr. Dionne again, only his secretary. To this day, I remain extremely puzzled about his motive in inviting me to Monaco. To surmise that he hoped to attract some of IATA's worldwide business to Monaco—perhaps a conference of some sort—is ridiculous, since I was a Very Unimportant Person. I can only suppose that he liked me during our brief conversation on the beach at Nice and wanted to treat me to a special holiday.

As I recount these IATA experiences, it comes to me that I must be one of the last surviving employees, if not the very last, from its early days. I make this observation on the grounds that, in the 1940s, most of us were in our twenties, and today those of us who are left are in our eighties.

I have always been grateful for my IATA experience. It not only included travel to many foreign cities, but it put me in touch with different cultures. I worked with the local airline people, sometimes explaining IATA's needs and policies to them, and receiving their feedback. I also enjoyed social occasions with them, visiting their homes and becoming acquainted with their families.

# Chapter 5

A<small>T SOME</small> point in my IATA years, I found myself thinking again about furthering my education. I used to wonder where Tom and I derived our desire for an education. The legal age for leaving school was fourteen, with the result that few of our friends in our working class neighbourhood went beyond Grade 8. They took jobs to help out with family finances. Certainly our parents never preached education to us but two incidents stand out in my mind. They were not significant in themselves, but they had huge implications for Tom and me. In Grade 10, Tom decided to produce a "newspaper" that he called the "Daily Hoot." It contained bits of school news, jokes, anecdotes, and, sometimes, reflections on the international situation, for the prospect of another world war was looming in the public mind. Production of the "Daily Hoot" was a messy, laborious task. Some details are hazy in my mind, but I do remember talk of a hectograph which involved a large tin tray (probably one of my mother's cake pans) that was filled with a violent purple liquid, said to contain Jello. Tom dipped his written sheets into this mixture, and produced a limited number of purple-coloured newspapers. When my parents noticed that Tom was neglecting his studies in favour of producing the "Daily Hoot," they threatened to withdraw him from school. I somehow knew that they were not serious, but he was stunned, and he gave up the "Daily Hoot." Today, it might be regarded as a creative endeavour.

As for me, I had my own agenda. I longed to quit school, and I begged my parents to allow me to take a job at Eaton's, the large department store in Montreal. Two of my friends were parcel girls there, meaning that they wrapped items all day long for $7.00 a week. Again, my parents were adamant. They insisted that we finish high school. So we studied the subjects that interested us—geography and history in Tom's case, English and history in mine—and we performed abysmally in subjects we didn't like. I believe that we could have both copped scholarships, but we didn't. Our parents must have breathed a huge sigh of relief when their wayward children graduated from high school. Had it not been for their insistence in this direction, our lives would have been much more limited.

At the time that Tom and I were seeking further education, we discovered Sir George Williams College (now Concordia University), which was crammed into two floors of the old Y.M.C.A. building in uptown Montreal. My enrolment in the evening degree program was a direct result of my attachment to Tom, and I give him full credit for awakening me to the beauties and promise of academic life.

Even now, I am amazed at the prescience of the college in providing a full-blown Evening Division to accommodate the educational needs of working students. Tom and I were delighted to learn that we could work for a living in the daytime and study for our degrees in the evening. I would finish my work at IATA and race to the college.

I managed my time so that I could, for example, enrol in a course on Tuesdays and Thursdays from 6:30 p.m.-8:30 p.m., and in a second course from 8:30 p.m.-10:30 p.m. My assignments were completed on weekends. Because of my frequent absences while working with IATA, I sometimes missed examinations or submitted late papers. As a result, my undergraduate transcript was spotty, showing deferred assignments and deferred grades that were subsequently redeemed.

Tom and I found ourselves among a group of highly motivated students working in the daytime and struggling at night to obtain their first degrees. The situation inspired a kind of camaraderie among us. We didn't feel sorry for ourselves. Rather, we enjoyed the unique opportunity provided for us. I am still astonished at the number of students, including Tom and me, who later obtained their doctoral degrees and made a real contribution to the society in which they lived. It was a great day when, finally, in 1950, we both earned the coveted bachelor's degree.

After seven years in IATA, I found the old restlessness asserting itself, or so it seemed. Actually, it took me a long time to realise that my boredom resulted from the fact that I wasn't fulfilling my potential, to use a favourite phrase of educators and others today. I had been using what writing talent I had to express Henry's ideas, and I wanted to try my hand at expressing my own ideas, however flimsy they might be. Also, I longed to attend university on a full-time basis without the distractions of a job. Many of my friends wondered aloud about my decision to leave IATA, unable to understand why I would surrender the opportunity to travel so extensively. I made the move with considerable foreboding, for I was facing an uncertain future. I knew that the time had come to strike out on my own, or I would find myself firmly on the road to a pension and a gold watch at the end of my labours.

I was plagued, as always, by my lack of confidence in my own ability. I have never envied other people their wealth, their prestige, their power, their beauty, or their talent, but I do envy people who have superb self-confidence. Sometimes it is justified, sometimes not. We all know people who, despite having no discernible talents or credentials, are nevertheless brimming with self-confidence. However, I applied to McGill University in Montreal, hoping to obtain a master's degree in English. To my utter dismay, my application was rejected, because of the lamentable appearance of my undergraduate transcript. I can still hear the voice of the crusty Scotsman who headed the McGill Department of English, proclaiming that my record represented "destitution." The word burned itself into my brain. (I never told him when, some years later, I was hired as a professor by McGill University.) The immediate problem posed by this rejection was that I would probably have to apply elsewhere and live away from home at considerable expense. The only way I could pay for this venture would be to cash in my IATA pension, which I did.

Having been soundly rebuffed by McGill University, I turned for help to Tom, then a high school teacher who had considerable knowledge of university programs. He advised me to apply to the University of Wisconsin at Madison, which boasted a stellar English faculty. I applied in 1953 to Wisconsin and, to my great relief and gratitude, I was accepted. But there were conditions. I was placed on probation and told that if I made up certain undergraduate courses, along with graduate courses, the "probation" label would be removed by Christmas. It was a challenge I couldn't resist.

During the year I spent at Wisconsin, I lived in a graduate residence, a large mansion that had belonged to Senator Vilas, who was a member of President Grover Cleveland's cabinet. The mansion had a vast library, with a breathtaking view of Lake Mendota, and a wonderful carved wooden staircase leading to the second floor. My room faced the lake, and I enjoyed watching the change of seasons, especially the dreamy fall days when the oak trees turned pure gold and the red maples flamed in the sunlight.

I quickly found myself at a considerable disadvantage in class, which included students about ten years younger than I and in possession of honours English baccalaureate degrees from acclaimed places like Smith College. I felt as though I had no business to attend classes with them, and I had little time for friendships, though I found one or two kindred spirits. The academic demands made upon me stretched my ability and my energy to their limits, but, thankfully, I completed all the requirements and I managed to shed the label "probation" by Christmas. While all this was going on, I experienced bouts of homesickness and some disorientation caused by the rather violent change from my totally different life in IATA.

It was with joy that, following the Christmas holidays with my family back in Montreal, I entered the second semester of study at Wisconsin and became a bona fide graduate student, even earning the respect of a fellow student, an honours English graduate from Smith College who had previously snubbed me.

The semester passed quickly, but I still had to complete two graduate courses, meaning that I would be enrolled for the summer. About this time, I was offered a fellowship to work on a doctorate. I declined it, partly because of my father's illness, but largely because the prospect of doctoral study was daunting. I returned to Montreal, deciding that I would spend the rest of my life as a high school teacher of English. To this end, I enrolled in the teacher training program at McGill University. I found the program a breeze, not nearly as arduous as the master's program at Wisconsin had been. I enjoyed working with the girls' classes during my practice teaching in Grades 8 and 9, although I made many mistakes. I thought I could communicate something of the excitement that filled me when reading poetry, and I even looked forward to teaching grammar, which was fascinating to me, though it is often considered a bore by other people. Ironically, at one point, I found myself placed as a student teacher with my one-time Grade 5 teacher, the ogre who had terrified me and my classmates with her harsh voice and harsher treatment of us. The horrors of my own schooling made me resolve to treat my future pupils with respect and kindness, while still demanding good performance from them!

# Chapter 6

I FINISHED THE year at McGill with honours and immediately found employment at Westmount Junior High School in the western part of Montreal. There, although I was 34 at the time, I found myself dealing with much older, experienced teachers who were set in their ways and suspicious concerning upstarts who arrived with new ideas about teaching. Much of the learning was rote, I discovered. I also discovered that, as a new teacher, I was given the most difficult Grade 9 class that no one else wanted to teach. This all-girl class contained a number of students who had been in various kinds of trouble. They were restless young women, standing tiptoe in the wings of the stage of life, excited yet apprehensive. Of the fourteen, nine had been runaways, several had records of disruptive school behaviour, and it was rumoured that several others had been prostitutes. One thing was certain: all were rejects, "throw-away" kids so far as the school and authorities, especially some teachers, were concerned. I found myself in the position of being expected to teach the high school curriculum to students who had not the slightest interest in becoming educated. By some miracle, they behaved themselves for me. Perhaps they sensed my insecurity and my sympathy toward them. I began to win them over when I discovered that romantic poetry appealed to them. I wowed them with Amy Lowell's "Patterns" and Alice Meynell's "Renouncement." Then I intermixed such poems with the "required" literature according to the curriculum. "Miss Tomkins, you are wonderful," exclaimed several students. I think I earned the grudging respect of the other teachers, to whom these students were throwaways, tolerated by the school until school-leaving age. However, in the eyes of these teachers, I made one big mistake when I permitted these students to have a party just before the Christmas holidays. I intended to keep the party a secret from the other teachers, but I forgot that my classroom was located directly above the female teachers' lounge, and the shuffle of the students' feet, as they danced, could be heard clearly. It took me a long time to live down my disgraceful behaviour, but I never regretted what I had done.

Another dilemma that I suffered related to two Grade 8 girls who caused a problem, not because they misbehaved, but because they worshipped me. During class, they sat at their desks, hands folded demurely in front of them, big blue eyes riveted on me. They hung on my every word and watched my every move. Frequently they misbehaved in class, with the intention that I would keep them after school! One day they brought a box of cheap jewellery, the result, I believed, of a raid on their mothers' hoard. I pondered what to do. I didn't want to spoil their fun, but neither did I want to accept stolen jewellery. Finally, I persuaded them to return the jewellery, and all was well.

The students in my other classes—the so-called "academic classes"—did well. Two of them, in fact, scored 100 in a stiff grammar test. Then, halfway through the second semester came a telephone call from McGill University, asking me if I would accept a position on the education faculty, from which I had graduated only months before. The only plausible reason for hiring someone with my very limited teaching experience lay in the anticipated surge in student enrolments as the baby boomers came of age. This offer involved a position at Macdonald College, the teacher training branch of McGill University, near the town of Ste. Anne de Bellevue, about 25 miles west of Montreal. I had always liked the campus, with its bucolic atmosphere, its green lawns sloping down to Lake St. Louis, and its substantial pink brick buildings topped by red roofs.

By this time, a change in my parents' circumstances had occurred which favoured the move to Macdonald College. While I was at IATA, my father had retired. He came home bearing two suitcases (the parting gift from the postal authorities) and wearing a bewildered expression. Barely a day passed before he declared, "I miss my job." What an irony it was that, after 25 years of working at a job he hated, he was sorry to give it up! It was at this point that the disparity between my parents' ages surfaced. My father relaxed in an armchair, wearing his slippers, and he urged my mother to join him. He was 65, and she was only 48. He wanted her to share in his old age, whereas she was still a vibrant woman, young for her age. She was interested in her garden, still sewing clothes for herself and for me, still cooking delicious meals, still following Canadian politics and world affairs. As always, she gracefully accepted her lot, and she continued doing her best to please my father. Fortunately, he liked to take long walks, and he was very good about doing errands for her. I believe that she thought up items in order to get him out of the house—a not uncommon reaction by wives when their husbands retire!

Gradually, my father's health deteriorated. By the time the offer came for me to teach at Macdonald College, it had become necessary to place him in a veterans' hospital, which, coincidentally, was located near the college. Given his adoration of my mother, it must have been terrible for him to be separated from her. She was upset when the supervising nurse commented that he had "a little weep each night". I used to visit him as often as I could, pushing him in his wheelchair around the grounds of the hospital in the sunshine. Some months later, my father died.

As I gazed at my father lying in his casket in the funeral parlour, I became aware that the organist was softly playing one of his favourite hymns, "The Old Rugged Cross." Also, I became suddenly fascinated by his folded hands. In a rush of memory, I recalled how, when I was little, those hands had lifted me in the air high above his head, as he smiled up at me. I also remembered that, when I was about two years old, those hands had held me on his lap while he opened a book of bedtime stories while some jelly beans dissolved into a sticky mess in my palm. And he had held my small hand comfortingly in his on that dreaded first day of school, when I left my babyhood behind and enrolled in Grade 1.

I think that there must always be some regret when we lose someone we have loved. The regrets that crowded into my mind, as I looked on my father's face, were that we hadn't given him the love, support, and patience that he badly needed after his harrowing experiences in World War I. Like many children, we were self-centred and not interested in a war that held little meaning for us. I know that, although he said little about his war experiences, he must have missed the camaraderie growing out of shared experiences with his fellow-soldiers in barracks, in trenches, and on the battlefields.

After my father died, my mother and I sold the Montreal house and bought a house a few miles from the college. I pass over the next ten years when I was teaching in the peaceful surroundings of Macdonald College. The adjacent small town of Ste. Anne de Bellevue consisted of venerable old homes, some of them constructed of stone, and small apartment buildings served by many small stores. It was, in many ways, an idyllic life. The faculty was small, consisting of seven professors, a number that was to swell in later years to hundreds, partly because the teaching profession became more attractive as a career choice. As a teacher, I was still a rank novice with much to learn, and I became a good, if not a brilliant teacher.

But, before the decade was over, I began to feel the old familiar itch for a challenge. I found an excuse in the realization that, if I were going to remain in university teaching, I should obtain a doctorate. My master's degree was already more than ten years old. In 1963, I decided, with great trepidation, to apply to Harvard University. I wondered at my own temerity, since I had always been in awe of Harvard, because of its prestige and long tradition. It was like reaching for the moon. I almost hoped they wouldn't accept me. On the other hand, I felt some excitement about living in Cambridge, which was next door to Boston, a city that I had visited on several occasions. I loved the city, because there is history in every stone, it is close to the sea, and it boasts many fine museums, art galleries, concert halls, restaurants, and several universities. Imagine my combined delight and terror when I was notified that Harvard had accepted my application!

## Chapter 7

ILOVED HARVARD from the moment that I set foot there. The New Yard contains Widener Library, which I used often. It houses over three million volumes and was built in memory of Harry Elkins Widener, who died on the *Titanic*. Facing it is the stately Memorial Church, commemorating Harvard alumni who had served in two world wars. In the Old Yard is a bronze statue of John Harvard, who had willed his library to the New College in the seventeenth century, just a few years after the Pilgrims had settled in the colony. New College was renamed Harvard College in his honour. On winter mornings, when his shoulders were dappled with snow, I used to say "Good morning, John Harvard" to him, whenever I passed by. I like to think that he smiled at me.

I had a lot of difficulty with my studies at Harvard. The courses were arduous, and the instructors were demanding, and I found myself burning a lot of midnight oil just to keep up with my studies. The standards were very high, and I began to wonder, that fall, whether I would survive, especially in a doctoral seminar that consisted of five students, including me. When my turn came to prepare a paper to read at the weekly meeting, I thought it was quite good. My instructor tore it apart, and I was crushed. Looking for a grain of comfort, I asked him, "is there anything good about my paper?" The answer was devastating. It was, he proclaimed, "industrious." The verdict could hardly have been worse. I nearly decided to pack up and return home. But defeat wasn't in my nature, and I resolved somehow to improve my performance.

About this time, I was befriended by another student, a handsome young man named Andre Fabia, whom I always think of as shining. I don't mean that he was my knight in shining armour, but that he literally shone from the top of his burnished head to his shoes that were so carefully shined as almost to be mirror-like. One night he called me to say, "Don't let Blackstock [the professor] get you down. He makes life difficult for every student. He thinks he's being rigorous." What a blessing his words were to me! I had been on the verge of leaving Harvard, and I felt reassured. What small, apparently insignificant circumstances can change one's life! In subsequent required papers, I wrote, rewrote, and wrote again until, gradually, the papers became clearer, more succinct, better organized.

Andre and I shared many a cup of coffee after that at the coffee shops that abound in Harvard Square. Later I learned, quite by accident, that he was gay. We kept in touch after I left Harvard in the summer of 1965. In fact, he wrote a letter when his spirits were low and his work was going poorly, and I replied with what I hoped were words of encouragement. Evidently, they helped him, because he replied, "I received your most wonderful letter. If you ever felt that you owed me anything, consider that debt paid." I wish that I had kept a copy of my letter. I hope it contained more than platitudes. In any event, it had the right effect.

By the end of my first year at Harvard, my funds were running low, even though I had obtained a Quebec Province scholarship, a Canada Council grant, and a Harvard scholarship. Accordingly, I took a part-time job for the summer at Wyeth Hall, the graduate women's residence where I lived. The Proctor was a woman from India who was studying city planning. She was noted for wearing colourful saris and preening herself before a mirror whenever the opportunity presented itself. As Assistant Proctor, I was paid a small sum of money and given dinner each night in the dining room in Radcliffe College. Otherwise, I could not have afforded dinner every night.

At Wyeth Hall, most residents were around 22 years of age and, thus, almost 20 years younger than I. The age difference didn't seem to matter to them. I was grateful that they embraced me as one of their own. I shared their joys and listened to their heartaches. Out of my own rich and varied life experience, I was sometimes able to help them. In effect, I became a kind of den mother, and I enjoyed the role.

In 1965, I faced a dilemma. I wanted to remain at Harvard to be near my advisor, Dr. Blackstock (who had become my friend), while writing my dissertation, but I couldn't afford to stay. Also, I was torn between returning to my professorship at McGill University or accepting an offer from the University of British Columbia (UBC) in Vancouver, Canada. I was afraid that, if I remained at Harvard for another year, the UBC opportunity would be lost. The incentive to join UBC was the presence of my brother Tom and his family in Vancouver.

I decided to accept the UBC position, and I arrived in Vancouver in the summer of 1965 with my mother, a move that was to change my life beyond my wildest imaginings. We left Montreal behind forever. From the first moment, I was enchanted with Vancouver. It seemed wonderful to me that I could teach at the university, drive a couple of miles to one of many beaches, have a refreshing swim, and drive downtown to shop within ten to fifteen minutes. Best of all was the climate. I was glad to escape the brutal winters, the snow and ice, of Eastern Canada, and the hot, humid summers. In Vancouver, the summers are fresh, rarely humid, and the temperature hovers between 70 and 80 degrees.

Tom was also on the UBC Education faculty, teaching social studies, and I enjoyed family life with him, his wife Doreen, and their four children. However, I was burdened with the double task of my teaching duties and the writing of my doctoral dissertation, which I had barely begun when I was at Harvard. Accordingly, I found myself in the frustrating situation of feeling that I wasn't doing a good job of teaching, because I was distracted by the dissertation, and I couldn't find the blocks of time needed to write it. It was about this time that Tom gave me a piece of advice that I have always treasured. "Forget having blocks of time," he said, "because they aren't going to happen. Learn to use small amounts of time productively." I heeded his advice. During lunch hour at the university, I would rush to the library to check one or two bibliographical references for my dissertation. When I arrived home in the late afternoon, I would use the half-hour or so before dinner to revise a clumsy sentence or to clarify an idea. To this day, I find myself still using small amounts of time effectively.

Later I faced another problem. I needed advice about writing the dissertation, but my advisor was 3,000 miles away, and the mail was slow. I envisioned myself an old woman still writing letters seeking advice. When Tom found me weeping over the situation, he shouted, "Write the damn thing, and sent it in to Harvard. They'll have to respond, and you'll get some direction." Despite my lachrymose state, I couldn't help smiling to myself over the fact that, when Tom most cared, he would appear angry.

# Chapter 8

IT WAS during this hectic period that I met John Niemi, the great love of my life. I attended a faculty Christmas party in the winter of 1966 and noticed that, whenever I moved, wherever I moved, the same man appeared at my shoulder. I wondered, of course, who he was, but paid little attention to him.

Shortly thereafter, preoccupied with the many demands facing me, I threw open the door to what I thought was my office. There, to my surprise, sat John. My office was directly beneath his, and I had unwittingly climbed an extra flight of stairs. I apologized, of course, and we talked for ten minutes. I learned that he had just passed the oral examination for his doctorate at the University of California—Los Angeles. I was thrilled to think that someone who was under the same pressure as I had actually finished! The next day he called and invited me to dinner. I told him solemnly that I had no time for dates and that my only social life consisted of having dinner at Tom's home on Sundays. Two weeks later, he telephoned with the same invitation. I repeated my answer.

I finished the dissertation and mailed it to Harvard shortly before Christmas, 1967. I felt that I should let John know, but I hadn't seen him or heard from him for many months. Then, on the day before Christmas Eve, I walked into the faculty mail room, and there stood John. "How's the dissertation coming?" he asked. 'It's finished," I replied, "and accepted." He shot back, "We'll have to celebrate. What are you doing for dinner tomorrow night?" This time, almost a year later, I accepted his invitation. It seems trite to say that we fell in love immediately, but that was true, and we remained in love for the next 35 years until he passed on in 2004. But I'm getting ahead of myself.

John's background was as different from mine as it is possible to imagine. I am sure that some people shook their heads over the disparity. He grew up in a noisy, engulfing, loveable family in a tightly knit Finnish community near Ironwood in the rural surroundings of Michigan's Upper Peninsula. It was settled largely by Finns, but there was a sprinkling of Italians and Corsicans. His grandparents were tenant farmers who came from Finland to America in the early 1900s out of a passionate desire to own their own land. They had heard that land was cheap and that there was work in the iron ore mines and in the woods in northern Michigan. In this new environment, they welcomed the sight of many birch trees, so reminiscent of Finland.

His grandparents were pioneers in every sense of the word. His grandmother wove her own wool to make stockings, other clothing, and incredibly heavy quilts. She milked the dozen cows that they kept, gathered eggs from the hens, separated the cream from the milk, and made butter to sell to the local dairy. At the same time, she raised ten children. In the absence of roads at the time, John's grandfather skied seven miles each day to the mine in the winter. Eventually both grandfathers died of black lung disease, induced by the iron ore dust.

It was a rough-and-ready macho culture, where men dominated and women were expected to be submissive although, as John pointed out, they had considerable informal power. They gave their opinions freely and sometimes prevailed in their arguments with the men. Most men worked in the iron ore mines, some in the woods, and others on county projects, such as roads, or in small businesses. As a boy, John put up snow fences at 75 cents per hundred feet, trapped weasels for their valuable ermine fur, logged in the woods, and fished for trout and salmon in nearby Lake Superior. In that society, shooting one's first buck was a rite of passage for young boys, and John liked to tell the story of how he went out in the morning as "Johnny" and, having shot his first buck, returned in the evening as "John."

John's prowess was all the more remarkable, because, at the age of six, he suffered a severe injury to his left knee. The accident occurred when he was playing in the classroom during recess on a rainy day. Evidently he climbed up onto a high window sill, slipped, and fell, jamming his knee in the coils of a radiator. The act of wrenching it away caused a grievous injury. Today, in an age when knee and hip replacements are almost commonplace, the knee could probably have been easily repaired, but, in the thirties, such procedures were unknown. John spent many years in braces and on crutches. Early snapshots show a little tow-headed boy on crutches, smiling gamely into the camera. It was a strange coincidence that both he and my father suffered a fractured left knee that left them with a permanent limp. As a relative remarked to me, John never showed any bitterness about his injury. Rather, it seemed to spur him on. He became an excellent dancer, and, while in Alaska, he completed the 26-mile marathon.

John idolized his father, and I think it is very likely that John would have followed him down into the mine, but for his injury. In fact, I said to him on one occasion, "I'm very far from saying what happened to you is a good thing, but, if it hadn't happened, I believe that you would have become an iron ore miner, and your life would have been much less interesting." An amusing anecdote relating to John's injured knee concerned his being drafted for service in the Korean War in 1951. John reported his stiff knee to the doctor. "Yeah," said the doctor caustically, "I've heard that excuse before." John responded, "Doc, if you can make this knee bend, I'll gladly go to Korea!"

By the time John's father grew up, the automobile had appeared on the scene, and he was able to drive each day to the mine. Mining was a hazardous occupation in those days, lacking the safety measures that were later developed, and John's mother worried constantly about the risk. Like her mother, she milked cows, sold butter and cream to the local co-op, and worked in the garden. Every day she washed her husband's mining clothes, watching the water run red with the iron ore dust.

The environment featured harsh winters, with an accumulation of snow amounting to 220 to 250 inches, and temperatures were often well below zero. Yet the mood was one of great cheerfulness and camaraderie. Perhaps the harsh environment united the people, for there was a strong sense of community as they helped each other. Since many families had intermarried, there were close kinship ties. Everyone was important, from the tiny baby to the great-grandmother, and people like me who married into those families were welcomed with open arms. The town hall was the hub of activity in the community. Any excuse was good for a celebration which always featured a vigorous accordionist who seemed to rip the music out of his instrument as he played the polkas, schottisches, and waltzes so dear to the hearts of the people. Another social center was the sauna that was part of every household. Some people had saunas installed in their basements. Others, like John's father, built what was called a "bathhouse" in the backyard. Cold water was thrown on rocks that had been heated to a high degree. Men and women sat on benches, enjoying the steam, but finding it so intense at times that they opened the door to let in some cool air. It took a little courage to run from the house to the bathhouse in below-zero temperatures with only a towel for protection. Gossip and political discussions were rife in the saunas.

A major concern in that community was a lack of rain in the summer. One can only imagine the intense anxiety with which the people scanned the summer skies for signs of rain that would ensure a bumper crop of hay for the cows during the winter. Men and women pooled their skills. Repair men were rarely called in to fix a car or a refrigerator, since, in that society, there was always someone who knew how to solve the problem.

This, then, was the society in which John grew up, and he remained nostalgic about it, even after the community that he loved gradually declined. The cause was the closing of the iron ore mines in 1965, due to the discovery of new, cheaper, and better grades of iron ore in places like Labrador. There were no pensions in those days for the miners, who had to fall back on the limited funds provided by Social Security. As the young people moved away from the Upper Peninsula of Michigan because of the lack of work, the population of Ironwood gradually diminished from 20,000 in the heyday of the mines to approximately 6,000. As young people left and businesses closed, an air of anxiety and despair crept over the community, and the old spirit withered.

John left his home to study for his bachelor's degree at Michigan State University in 1951. Then he responded to the lure of Alaska, one of the last frontiers and one that rewarded young people who were willing to live and work there. He found a community much like the one he had left. Again, the sense of community was born of the need for people to draw together in the face of a harsh environment. He had a picture of a thermometer in Fairbanks that registered 58 degrees below zero in the winter. In addition to the cold, the winter days were short and very dark, with something over two hours of daylight. In the summer, the days were much longer. It was still bright at two in the morning. In Alaska, John pursued his master's degree from the University of Alaska, became Assistant to the President and, later, Director of Evening and Off-Campus Courses. There, working with functionally illiterate adults in the armed forces, he developed his lifelong commitment to adult education.

John left Alaska in 1964 to earn his doctorate at the University of California—Los Angeles, and subsequently moved to Vancouver, Canada, where he accepted a position at UBC. He soon found out that he knew little about Canada—its history, its culture, its politics, especially the parliamentary system of government—and he spent long hours in the library. His search for knowledge was spurred on by such remarks from the students as "Don't give us any of that Yankee stuff." He quickly became known as a professor who cared deeply about his students and who reached out into the community as few Canadian professors did at that time. Rather, it was the custom, with some exceptions, for professors to remain at the university and to expect the world to come to them.

The disparity between our backgrounds was rivalled

by the disparity between our temperaments. I had never met anyone like him, with his bounding energy, his goodwill toward everyone, and his rare blend of intellectual strength and practical skills learned while logging, fishing, hunting, and trapping in his youth. As my sister-in-law remarked, "John seizes life with both hands." He made friends wherever he went. As one person said to me, "No one who met John ever forgot him." The old cliché about the attraction between opposites rang true for us. I had never known anyone so vigorous, so passionate about everything he did, especially his teaching. It is fair to say that John streaked like a meteor across the placid landscape of my life. His style was utterly foreign to my own sedate, rather starchy upbringing. The importance placed on good speech and manners often caused people in my society to conceal their true feelings or at least to express them in acceptable ways. I had often rebelled against this repression by raising controversial matters and by questioning the cautious, complacent tenor of Canadian life.

My family didn't quite know what to make of John. They had never met anyone like him. But I was smitten. I found him irresistible from the beginning. He quickly made most of the men I knew seem effete and uninteresting. With John I felt released and free, like a bird that has burst from its egg. He made me feel not only loved as a woman, but valued and worthy as a person, a new experience for me. My self-confidence didn't exactly zoom, but it improved greatly. For his part, I think that he was fascinated by me, because I was different from the women he had known in Ironwood and Alaska, where he had lived for ten years.

Our romance flourished. I think that, with our doctorates in hand after much hard work, we wanted to make up for the lost social life of the past several years. Also, we discovered that both of us had had unique, varied life experiences far beyond those of many adults in our age group. John shared his Alaska, Michigan State, and University of California experiences with me. He also shared his varied work experience during the summers, including a stint as a short-order cook at a Wisconsin resort. With no experience, he bought a chef's hat and apron and sallied forth to toss hamburgers on a grill and to rise at 4:00 a.m. to create huge bowls of coleslaw. He worked at a clothing store one summer, and infuriated the other employees by his success in persuading customers to buy ties, shirts, suits, pants, and jackets.

On our first date, we tore across the Lion's Gate Bridge to attend a movie, "Far From the Madding Crowd," in West Vancouver, followed by dinner. I soon realized that this hectic experience foreshadowed the course of my married life. John was chronically late and always in a hurry. I liked to settle in church ten minutes before the service began, but we usually arrived, breathless, when the congregation was already singing the first hymn. On one notable occasion, we arrived late for a flight to Vancouver from Chicago's O'Hare Airport. As we sprinted down the corridor, late as usual, I secretly hoped that we would miss the plane, so that he might learn a lesson. We arrived to find the gate deserted, except for the ticket agent, who informed us that he had to let our seats go. "However," he said cheerfully, "we have a couple of first class seats for you." John remarked, "Isn't this nice?" as he settled into his seat, and I formally renounced any hope of changing his habits. What can I do, I thought, when the angels fight on his side!

To return to our courtship, we were ready for marriage and yet we were somewhat cautious about entering unfamiliar territory. John was 36, and I was 46, and we had both been on our own for a long time. I had given up any thought of marriage, surmising that most of the eligible men were gone. All that remained, I reasoned, were gay men or men carrying the baggage of ex-wives and children. And, always, the recollection of my mother's plight and my distrust of men lingered in the shadows of my mind.

But John was different, and soon we found ourselves engaged in a flurry of affectionate cards which we whizzed every day under each other's office door. Then, when the academic year ended in May, 1968, John left to give a workshop at Ocean Shores, Washington. From there he traveled to California to see his old friend, Professor Jack London, to whom he announced that he had found his girl at last and was going to be married—something he had not told me. In the meantime, I had decided that, if he called me immediately upon his return, I would say "yes." I tried to calm myself by reflecting that, if he didn't call, I would get on with my life, enjoying my work, my friends, my family, and my church. But, to my joy, he called immediately upon his return and, from then on, it was merely a question of setting the wedding date.

We were married on December 11, 1968, at the beginning of the university's three-week Christmas holiday. We married against the wishes of my widowed mother. She objected to John's Finnish background, because it was "ethnic." She never considered that she, too, was "ethnic." But the real reason for her opposition, I believe, was her understandable fear of being left alone at nearly 70, when she had expected (as indeed I did, too) that I would remain with her for the rest of her life. John said, "Don't worry about your mother. I'll win her over." And he did, by taking her to places she wanted to visit and lavishing gifts and money on her.

I came to marriage as a virgin. Like most women of my generation, I had been raised to believe that premarital virginity was important, and I continued to think so after I examined this proposition independently. To defend these restrictions may sound impossibly idealistic or even unrealistic, but I honestly believe that, when two people who truly love and are committed to each other marry, and experience sex for the first time, it becomes a physical affirmation of a deeply felt spiritual union. It has been called "a kissing of the bloods," and people who cheapen this experience by making it one of a series of such encounters, often without love or commitment, miss out on some of life's most rewarding, joyous moments. For me, marriage was immensely fulfilling. I had not known passion, or even understood it, and so I was unprepared for the deep well of passion I discovered in myself, unprepared for my joy in the urgent thrust of his body as it sought my secret passage. I understood commitment and was prepared to give it in full measure. The combination was wonderful. Passion without love and commitment seems empty to me.

We quickly forged a professional partnership. As a professor of English, I had developed certain writing skills, which I had had in rudimentary fashion since childhood, and I lent my talents to John's career as a professor of adult education. In addition, we shared a deep religious faith, and we honestly tried to live our lives by Christian principles of love toward our fellow men. We didn't always succeed. Sometimes we would point out to each other certain flaws in our behaviour, such as being mean-spirited, petty, or selfish. The process wasn't always a happy one. It isn't pleasant to be told that one has acted insensitively, if not boorishly. In effect, we became each other's best friend and severest critic.

An interesting facet of John's personality was his silence when facing stressful situations. I recall an occasion when he approached the dean to fund a certain project that was close to his heart. The dean replied that all the funds for the year had been allocated. Many people would have erupted in protest, but not John. I watched him. His body slumped ever so slightly, and his face bore a wounded expression, but he said nothing. Facing this uncomfortable silence, the dean hesitated. Then he said, "Leave it with me, John. I'll see what I can do." Sure enough, a few weeks later, the funds came through. On another occasion, when I was ranting and raving over some grievance, I became aware that he was looking at me silently—not fighting back, not reproving me, but simply watching me. I felt ashamed of my rage and verbosity. To this day, I have never decided whether John's silence was an unconscious response or a conscious strategy. Either way, his silence worked!

# Chapter 9

JOHN AND I stayed at UBC for another seven years. We had some happy family times with my mother, Tom, his wife Doreen, and their four children. The many fine beaches and parks of Vancouver were ideal for picnics, swimming, and hiking. However, John was chafing at the arbitrary behaviour of his department head, and he felt the need for more freedom. So it was that, when John was offered a position at Northern Illinois University in 1975, we accepted. It was with considerable reluctance that we left Vancouver and moved to the small university town of DeKalb, Illinois. It is situated sixty miles west of Chicago and is surrounded by cornfields. For me, the move to DeKalb was a major one that involved leaving my family, my friends, my job, my church, and my country. For John, it was going home to an environment that better suited his exuberant, free-wheeling style and his wide-ranging interests. In other words, he was much better suited to the American scene than to the staid, laid-back Canadian scene. Somewhat to my surprise, I, too, found myself much better suited to the earthy, vibrant American scene. Also, my rather cautious nature was transformed by John's irrepressible optimism. "There are no problems, only opportunities," he would proclaim.

This attitude seemed to me to express the decidedly American qualities of vitality and ingenuity that I came to admire during my thirty years in the United States.

We didn't divorce ourselves completely from Canada. In fact, John's Canadian colleagues liked and admired him. This fact became evident from the summer teaching assignments that he was offered at five Canadian universities, even after he moved to the States. This development was all the more surprising in view of the thinly veiled, sometimes virulent anti-American sentiment that clouds the otherwise tolerant Canadian character.

In DeKalb, we rented an apartment near the campus and began the slow process of finding new friends and familiarizing ourselves with the local shops, restaurants, and limited cultural resources. We were thrilled to find in the town the Egyptian Theatre, one of only a few remaining edifices of that kind. It was built in the 1920s at the height of the Egyptology craze, set off by the discovery of King Tutankhamen's tomb in the Valley of the Kings by Howard Carter and Lord Carnarvon in 1922. Art Deco in style, the lobby of the theatre is large and cavernous with a high ceiling and a floor consisting of black-and-white tiles. Statues and drawings of Egyptian pharaohs are scattered throughout the lobby and the theatre itself. It is the site of plays and concerts, and it is the home of the Kishwaukee Symphony Orchestra. The orchestra is peopled by many members of the Northern Illinois University Music Department, which has an excellent reputation.

As a person who had lived and worked in the great cities of the world, I was ill-prepared for life in a small town. But, as the months progressed, I began to appreciate its advantages. I noticed that the traffic was slow, the pace unhurried, the manner friendly. People paused for leisurely conversations on street corners, in the grocery store, in the bakery, and in other small shops. Perhaps these are the features that prompt many people to settle in small towns, content to make a modest living. We knew a bright, personable young man named Rich, who had opened a small store, much like the old five-and-dime-store. Crammed into the limited space were bolts of fabric, ribbon and thread in all colours of the rainbow, gaudy T-shirts, paper doilies, greeting cards, artificial flowers, fresh flowers displayed in a large glass case and a variety of jewelry. Likewise, many doctors, dentists, lawyers, accountants, and other professional people seemed satisfied to practice in a small town with a relaxed pace and relatively low overhead costs, and they tailored their fees accordingly. On more than one occasion, our lawyer said, "We'll let that go. I won't charge you for it." We knew two surgeons, husband and wife, who deliberately chose to live in DeKalb because they wanted to conduct their business and raise their children in a small town, with its air of innocence and tranquility, free of the hassles and temptations of big-city life.

One summer afternoon, we attended a function that seemed to me to be quintessential small-town America. It was an ice-cream social, held on the spacious lawns of the Ellwood House, a nineteenth century mansion. As the band played lively tunes on the broad cement terrace, people strolled in leisurely fashion on the lawn beneath the large shade trees, pausing to converse with friends and neighbours, and sitting at tables to consume ice cream and cake. As I watched people enjoying the festivities, I understood why those raised in small towns often speak of their childhood and youth with dreamy-eyed nostalgia.

Another activity that John and I enjoyed in our small

town was the annual Corn Fest, held on the last weekend of August. Corn Fest celebrates the bountiful harvest
produced by the corn fields that ring the city. Each year
the Del Monte company, which has a large plant in the
city, donates a seemingly endless supply of corn to the
townsfolk. There was an air of conviviality as people sat
on lawn chairs or on the curbs in the town square, slath-
ering butter on their corn and conversing while keeping
a watchful eye on children enjoying the big Ferris wheel
and the various rides. The downtown streets were closed
to traffic, so that people could wander freely among
stands offering hot dogs, hamburgers, barbecued pork,
and soft drinks. Merchants seized the opportunity to
rid themselves of surplus summer merchandise, offering clothing and other items at big discounts. In the large
parking lot, bands play constantly, and we joined in the
dancing. On Saturday morning, people were challenged
to run races or simply walk a distance ranging from one
to eight kilometres. We always did the 1km walk, usually bringing up the rear—"carrying the lantern," as John
called it. Water was supplied along the route and, at the
end, walkers and runners enthusiastically feasted on
slices of orange, cantaloupe, and apple. Always, on this
festive occasion, the sun shone brightly in the heavens.

John had always thrown himself passionately into his
work. Now he was caught up in new demands in a new
setting. They challenged even his almost super-human
energy. It was not unusual for him to put in a 21-hour
day, arising at 4:00 a.m. to read student papers, attending all-day meetings or driving to classes in Chicago. He
would arrive home, his eyes smudged with fatigue, but
still smiling, still demanding, "Where's my hug? Where's
my kiss?" But I began to feel neglected, especially since
John devoted extra time to individual students and spent

many hours intervening on their behalf with recalcitrant university officials. "Don't fret," he would say, "because the students are our bread and butter." I agreed, but I felt more lonely than at any time in my life. I needed friends, and it takes time to find them in a new setting.

I also felt the need for intellectual stimulation, and I began teaching writing courses as an adjunct professor, at Northern Illinois University. Some graduate students in adult education began asking for individual help, and the number slowly increased as more students sought assistance in writing their doctoral dissertations. I found this field more interesting than my own field of English, because it embraced students of all ages, from 25 to 60, from all kinds of different backgrounds and with different life histories and ambitions. There were community college teachers, training directors in business and industry, nurses, and consultants in the corporate world. It was wonderful to work with such a range of students and to listen to their hopes, dreams, and plans. Some wrote very well, and some wrote so badly that I wondered how they had gotten so far. The blunt fact was that the doctoral dissertation was the first major piece of writing that many of them had undertaken. A majority of them had never had systematic instruction in writing, unless you count a long-ago course in freshman English. It was rewarding to work with these students and to watch their progress as they learned to set forth a clear purpose and stay with it, to clarify the concepts they were using, to impose coherence on convoluted sentences, to marshall and sustain arguments, and to supply the needed emphasis. I didn't get any pay for this work, but I figured it was good for my head to wrestle with problems of style and substance, and I enjoyed the lively interaction with the students. Also, I reasoned that I was making a small contribution to society. I received gifts I wasn't expecting, including lunches, dinners, and flowers. An African-American student, a middle-aged man whom I helped, gave me an exquisite gold maple leaf pin in acknowledgment of my Canadian heritage. Most welcome of all were the letters of gratitude that I received.

John would read the dissertations to me, and we would discuss their good points and their weaknesses. I always tried to say something positive, even when it was a struggle to do so, before launching into a discussion of what needed to be corrected. I became so proficient at listening that, when we reached page 60, for example, I would recollect that, around page 40, the student had stated a different purpose. In other words, there was a problem of inconsistency.

In DeKalb, John rediscovered his Finnish roots, especially since he had moved much closer to his old home in Upper Michigan, about 400 miles distant. When we visited John's hometown, I had to sort out all the relationships among John's large, noisy, engulfing family. His grandmother had borne ten children, and so there was a proliferation of aunts, uncles and cousins. I learned to overlook some of their crudities, and I came to love them for their merry, uninhibited approach to life.

Also, John discovered a thriving Finnish community in DeKalb, centered at the Bethlehem Lutheran Church, the Finnish Labor Temple, and the Finn Hall. In the old days, the basement of the Finn Hall had housed young Finnish immigrants who came to work in the barbed wire factory and the Wurlitzer factory in DeKalb. I found that, in order to enter this life, I had to learn to dance fast polkas, schottisches, and waltzes. The fun-loving Finns in both DeKalb and Ironwood loved their polkas in particular. It was a different world to me, and I entered it with joy. We visited John's home as often as we could, always at Thanksgiving, which opened the hunting season. The woods rang with gunshots. Inevitably, there were accidents, because some hunters shot at anything that moved. The brother of John's best friend was killed in just such a way.

John's parents' home was humble. It was constructed from wood that his father had salvaged from the old school house, which he purchased for a dollar in 1930 and tore down to create a home for himself and his bride. In the back porch, he installed the old iron school bell that weighed about 200 pounds. As in most Finnish homes, the kitchen was the most important room, always featuring a large table to accommodate the many visitors who dropped in for coffee. The Finns of Upper Michigan are famous for their hospitality, and the coffeepot was always at the ready. At Christmastime, the tiny house was crowded to the walls with relatives and friends, always ready to laugh and joke.

After we moved to Illinois, my mother visited us each year for two months in the spring and two months in the fall. Remarked one of John's colleagues, "You must have some kind of tolerance. I won't have my mother-in-law for more than a week!" My mother underwent a remarkable change when she visited us. Her life in Vancouver was limited to keeping house, shopping, and seeing the family and a few friends. As a person who had "done" for other people all her life, she thrived on becoming part of our DeKalb household. She banished me from my kitchen, so that she could make bread and pastries, and she tackled with zest the pile of mending that always awaited her. She also developed a new social life in DeKalb and a circle of admirers among our friends. I was amused by an encounter with one of John's colleagues, who asked this little old lady, in a somewhat patronizing manner, "What books have you read lately?" He was somewhat taken aback when she replied, "I've been enjoying Theodore White's In Search of History."

An incident that occurred during one of my mother's visits to DeKalb stands out vividly in my memory. A friend of mine was about to be married, and my mother commented, as she had done in the past, about the folly of marriage for women. I had long ago discerned this vein of bitterness in her, and I found myself saying, "When are you going to drop that burden that you have carried all these years? You had a good husband who loved you, and you have two great children." She said not a word, but arose quietly and left the kitchen to return to her room. Now I've done it, I thought. About an hour later, my mother reappeared, and we resumed our companionable ways. Not a word was said about the incident then, or ever after, but I like to think I made a difference.

John and I spent many hours in fabric stores with my mother while she pounced with glee on buttons at ten cents a card and bought fabrics and patterns. Also, we took many trips from DeKalb, some when John was visiting another university, some on purely social grounds. Once, I recall that, while in Iowa City, we looked around for something to do in the evening. I noticed that the movie, "The Man Who Would be King," was playing at a local theatre. "I think that's Kipling's novel," I said, "and, if it is, it will be a rousing adventure yarn." And so it turned out to be, as well as an excellent psychological study of a man who believed in the myth of his own omnipotence and was destroyed by it. History is replete with such characters.

The proximity of DeKalb to Chicago was a boon. Whenever possible, we spent weekends in that vibrant city, shopping, attending concerts, plays, and world-class exhibits. Among them were the King Tutankhamen exhibit and the *Titanic* exhibit, which included a three-ton section of the ship's hull, with glass portholes intact, and many objects rescued from the wreck. The items included a gold necklace, a lady's silver dance slipper, and assorted blue-and-white dishes. I had been fascinated by the *Titanic* story since childhood. A friend showed me a small book containing pictures (in sepia brown) of the grand staircase, the ballroom, the dining-rooms, the staterooms, and the card room. Class lines were strictly drawn, and the first-class passengers rejoiced in their opulent surroundings, while those of humble origin (many of them immigrants) languished below deck. I have a picture in my mind of those poor folk crying out and beating vainly on the locked door of the steerage area, as the *Titanic* slowly sank and half-filled lifeboats drew away from the doomed ship. After these spectacular exhibits, the Cleopatra exhibit seemed rather tame, despite the presence of the glittering gold dress that Elizabeth Taylor wore in the movie. We learned something that we hadn't known before—that there were seven Cleopatras in all.

Having rediscovered his Finnish roots in Ironwood, John felt an intense desire to visit Finland, where he became a Fulbright scholar in 1981. He was much perturbed when he discovered that I had no intention of accompanying him. Simply put, I realized that I would probably spend the four months, from September to December, alone in a Helsinki apartment in the dark, cold Finnish winter, while he dashed around the country giving lectures, conducting research, and consulting. I reasoned that he would be better off without having to worry about me, and it turned out that I was right.

During our time in DeKalb, John organized and conducted study tours for faculty and students to Canada, Finland, Russia, and the Netherlands. He held the firm belief that faculty and students should experience adult education beyond the borders of their own country. In Finland, he made it possible for them to reside at a folk school named Vitta Kivi and to hear lectures at the University of Helsinki. Also, he arranged for them to hear lectures at the University of Leningrad (now St. Petersburg) in the then Soviet Union. Sometimes I accompanied him on these trips, sometimes not. The hectic pace was too much for me.

The following few years brought a train of sorrows. John's father died in Ironwood in 1983, his mother in mid-April, 1985, Tom in late April of the same year, and my mother in late July.

Tom was only 65, a rather young age in those days. His life had been interesting.  When he finished high school, he, like me, went to work in a bank, but the routine seemed mundane. When he expressed an interest in teaching, my parents could hardly contain their joy. In those days, it was possible to obtain a teaching certificate after just one year of training. Soon Tom found himself teaching in elementary school in Verdun, a working-class suburb of Montreal, where we were living at the time. Later he progressed to high school teaching and then to an administrative post as vice-principal of Verdun High School. In the meantime, he had become a fervent socialist, joining the Co-operative Commonwealth Federation (CCF), now the New Democratic Party. For a time, he and some close friends embraced Soviet Communism with great enthusiasm. They saw it as a revolt of the common man against the abuses of capitalism. But their high idealism soon evaporated when faced with the excesses of the Stalinist regime. It soon became evident that this regime was at least as oppressive as the Tsarist regime it had replaced. Tom never ran for office, but he did manage an unsuccessful campaign of the socialist candidate in Verdun. I decided to help my brother by distributing handbills in the district.

Later, in 1953, he applied for and won a British Council scholarship that took him to the University of London in England. There he met and married Doreen Gregory, also a student, who shared his keen interest in geography. They came to Montreal in 1954, and he resumed his position as vice-principal. But the year in London had revived his interest in teaching, and he became increasingly restless over his administrative duties. Then, in 1960, out of the blue one day came an offer from UBC to teach geography in the Faculty of Education, which he accepted. Later, he received his doctorate from the University of Washington.

The death of Tom, my only sibling, was hard for me to accept. The day before his death, with his wife and children at his bedside, under the glaring lights in a stark, white hospital room, he asked to see me alone. He was lucid. He looked at me, smiled, and said, "We've both been over-achievers, haven't we?" I nodded. I couldn't speak. My mind was numbed by the realization that our long, affectionate, sometimes scrappy relationship was coming to an end and that we were saying goodbye. When I recovered my voice, I told him how much I loved him and how grateful I was to him for guiding me over the years through the academic mazes that confronted me. "You have been an inspiration to me for most of my life," I said. He looked pleased, smiled, and closed his eyes. He died the next day with the family again at his bedside. Earlier, he had called John in Illinois to say goodbye, an act that left John so traumatized that he could not speak of it for many weeks without choking on his words. The anguish on my mother's face, as she watched her firstborn draw his last breath, is etched indelibly on my memory. She looked like a wounded bird that had lost the strength and the will to fly. It occurred to me, then, that the worst tragedy in life is the loss of a child, because it defies the natural order. A parent does not expect to outlive a child. The second is desertion by a partner (often through divorce), because it frequently involves not only a sense of loss, but also a sense of rejection, even betrayal. The third is the death of a partner.

I was not surprised when my mother died three months later. Our family believed that Tom's death was too much for her to handle at the age of 86. At the last, as I gazed on her work-worn hands and her small, still form as she lay on the hospital bed, I marvelled at how loving she had been, how rock steady as she guided all of us through the outer storms, and I thanked her silently.

After the sorrows of 1985, our spirits were lifted and we felt blessed when the announcement came, in the spring of 1986, that the University of Helsinki had awarded John an honorary Doctorate of Philosophy degree. So it was that we traveled to Helsinki for the "Promotio," a ceremony held every five years for the purpose of bestowing honorary doctorates on 25 international scholars who were considered to have made significant contributions to Finnish language, culture, and education. The celebrations included a round of elegant balls, solemn ceremonies in the great cathedral, a cruise on the Baltic, and a week spent in Helsinki's luxurious Marski hotel. At the conclusion of these festivities, the Finns proclaimed, "John, you are no longer an American. You're one of us." It was a thrilling moment for him. The fact that he had been born on Finnish Independence Day, December 6, further endeared him to the Finns. On the night of December 6, 1987, when he was traveling through the countryside, almost every house was aglow with blue candles in the windows in celebration of Finnish independence. A Finnish friend remarked, "Look, John, they're celebrating your birthday!"

At the conclusion of the Promotio festivities, we flew to London for a month's stay. A memorable experience was our attendance at the Sunday service in Westminster Abbey. At that service, coincidentally, the new mayor of the City of Westminster was installed. We stayed to listen to the organ music that resounded through the old cathedral, and we lighted votive candles, as we had in Helsinki, in memory of John's parents, my mother, and my brother. We emerged in the sunlight to hear the joyous pealing of bells. We then took a taxi to the Cheshire Cheese, an eighteenth century dining place that was a favourite of Dr. Samuel Johnson, whom I had long admired as a poet and as the writer of a famous dictionary. Our last stop that day was St. Paul's Cathedral, which contains the crypts of the Duke of Wellington, Lord Nelson, and Sir Christopher Wren.

While in England, we had a rather sweet experience when we visited Milton Keynes, site of the Open University, which captured John's interest as an adult educator. At the hotel, we inquired about places to eat and were told that the Tawny Owl pub served good food. Following directions, we started across the meadows that stretched serene and golden under the late afternoon sun. They seemed to shimmer and float as a gentle breeze fanned the grass. Soon we were joined by two lonely little girls, aged ten and seven, who had lately moved from London to Milton Keynes. They offered to take us to the pub and, during our short walk, they were enchanted to learn that we were Americans, the first such creatures they had met. It turned out that their chief interest in America lay in a burning desire to visit Disneyland. When we reached our destination, we parted, but not before John gave a ten-dollar bill to the older girl. She was as excited as if we had bestowed a fortune on her. "Do you mean it?" she inquired wonderingly, holding the bill aloft between her fingers. Then the two of them scampered across the fields, bound for home, where their parents no doubt scolded them for talking to strangers. The vignettes I have described illustrate two rare, idyllic days we enjoyed that did much to lift our spirits after the sad events of 1985.

On another occasion, when we were in Europe, we visited the then Soviet Union, when John taught at the University of Leningrad. We had supposed that the Russians would be cold and rather suspicious, but we found them to be warm and friendly. We had our own driver and interpreter. The driver, Vladimir, spoke no English. He seemed to be some kind of Communist party functionary. We deduced this because, every day when we were on our way to the university, a restaurant, (or, on one occasion, the ballet), he had a way of disappearing into the Communist headquarters bearing a portfolio that he left there. Our interpreter was a woman who liked to talk about the "Great Patriotic War," as the Russians dubbed World War II. Such was the influence of these two individuals that, when we expressed a desire to attend a ballet performance, they drove us to the theatre, marched us to the head of a long line, and installed us in seats overlooking the stage. We felt embarrassed about being swept to the front of the line.

Since both of us were interested in Russian history, we were thrilled to visit Smolny, which contained the offices occupied by Lenin, Stalin, and Trotsky following the 1917 Revolution. It was an impressive building, rather shabby, that had served as the Communist Party headquarters. There Lenin, Stalin, and Trotsky planned the new society that would replace Tsarist rule. One of their decrees involved establishing state ownership of the land, seizing the great estates of the nobles of the Tsar's court. Ironically, Smolny had been a school for the daughters of the nobility under the Tsar, and Lenin's office still bore a metal sign that read "Class Mistress." What an ideological shift!

During the Smolny visit, we were shadowed by a dour-appearing man who claimed to be an historian. John said quietly to me, "Be careful what you say. He's probably a KGB agent." Unwittingly, I blew his cover when I asked him for the name of the Tsar's fourth daughter. I knew the names of three of his daughters and his son, but the name of the fourth daughter eluded me. To my amazement, he didn't know her name. Perhaps it was too much to expect an historian to remember such a trivial item, but I thought he should! The other interesting feature of Smolny was the sparsely furnished apartment that had housed Lenin and his wife Krupskaya.

Our interest in historic sites led us to one of the most unsettling experiences of our lives. John and I were invited to West Berlin in the mid-1980s to attend two seminars—one in East Berlin, one in West Berlin—on adult education in the divided country of Germany. When the seminars ended, we travelled to Munich, and decided to visit nearby Dachau, one of the many infamous death camps in Nazi Germany. Evidently General Eisenhower had decreed that the camp was to be left in its original state, instead of being dismantled, so that future generations would realise the enormity of Nazi barbarism.

One of many gloomy buildings that housed the prisoners featured rows of bunks, one on top of another, extending as high as the eye could see. I noticed that the once smooth steps leading to the upper bunks had been hollowed out by the feet of countless prisoners. Next to this building, conveniently close, were the gas chambers, featuring ostensible shower-heads in the ceiling that dispensed not water, but deadly gases, to the unsuspecting prisoners. Still another building contained the names, and sometimes the photographs, of the thousands who had perished at Dachau. When we finally emerged from the camp, passing the high watch towers that guarded the gates, we didn't speak. As we drove off in our small Volkswagen bus, our silence continued for some time as we struggled to deal with the horrifying record set before us.

Our other travels yielded happier experiences. We especially enjoyed travelling to Canada for summer school teaching. These assignments brought carefree weeks as teaching his classes was the only demand placed on John. He didn't have to attend the endless meetings and conform to the bureaucratic requirements that were features of his life at Northern Illinois University. I remember, with particular pleasure, our visit to Halifax, where we discovered the graves of some *Titanic* victims and studied large-scale maps of the convoys that constantly steamed out of Halifax to protect merchant ships on their voyages across the Atlantic during World War II. We had an amusing experience when we asked to see photographs. The librarian admitted, rather sheepishly, that the lady who looked after them was on vacation and that the references to those materials were housed in incomprehensible fashion in shoe boxes. "There's one lady," remarked my husband, "who doesn't have to worry about being fired!"

During another summer, we stayed in Montreal, where John was teaching at Concordia University in the heart of the city. This occasion gave me the opportunity to renew my old friendship with Kitty and to learn the details of her life since we finished high school. Like me, she had an interesting history to relate. As previously mentioned, Kitty worked as a baby-nurse for some time in India. While living in Hyderabad, she attended a dance, and met a young British lance-corporal with the impressive name of Granville Armstrong-Whitworth. They were married within six months, and soon found themselves travelling to East Africa. "The life of a soldier's wife isn't easy," Kitty said to me, "because you have to be prepared to pack up and move at a moment's notice." She recounted a time when she found herself sitting alone in a crude wooden cart, drawn by a bullock, surrounded by various family possessions, with a child on her lap and another one growing within her.

In all, she had three children, all of them boys. When World War II broke out, Gran was posted to England, a move that Kitty welcomed as she had close relatives there. Finally, it seemed she had a permanent home. However, when demobilization came at the end of the war, Kitty and Gran and their three boys returned to Canada, where they lived on a slim military pension and such security positions as Gran could obtain. During her period in England, I lost track of Kitty. In the meantime, I was making such significant life-changes that she would have had a hard time tracking me down. Fortunately, she remembered that Tom was living in Vancouver and she contacted him. So, after many years apart, we finally got together, to our great joy. I found her little changed after the momentous events of her life. She was still the same cheerful girl I had known and loved in high school. Our lives had gone in vastly different directions, yet somehow the years fell away, and we were back on the old footing.

During our visit, I learned that Gran had been very much afraid of meeting John, because John was an academic and Gran had had little education. John soon put him at his ease by talking about his experiences with the military in Alaska. A few years later, Gran died. Afterwards, I visited Kitty several times in Montreal. Kitty died two years ago, very peacefully, after a brief illness.

Back in DeKalb, John discovered that no adult education programs were available to Navy personnel and civilians at the Great Lakes Training Center (the largest facility of its kind in the world) some hundred miles distant. He talked various Navy and university officials into offering courses that would enable Navy personnel (who were required to sign up for twenty years, after which they received a pension) to re-enter civilian life with degrees that would serve them well. Some of them retired as early as 40, and so could look forward to pursuing other interests for many more years. During this period, John was awarded the coveted titles of "Distinguished Teaching Professor" at Northern Illinois University and "Outstanding Teaching Professor" at the University of California—Los Angeles.

In 2001, John's contributions to Finnish education and culture culminated in his being awarded the title "Commander of the Order of the Lion of Finland," that country's highest civilian honour. Again, we were invited to Helsinki to receive this award, but John's health was beginning to fail. Instead, the Finnish Ambassador to the United States flew from Washington to Chicago for the ceremony. We were permitted to invite 40 people to attend it.

By this time, we had been married for 31 years. We still rejoiced in each other's company, and we still had a passionate relationship. However, in 1998, John underwent heart bypass surgery, followed by a diagnosis of diabetes. Whether there was a causal connection I will never know. The diabetes caused complications that led to his collapse one night in January 2004. He was taken to hospital, never to return home. Subsequently, he was moved to several Chicago hospitals over a period of five months. I became almost accustomed to occupying the passenger seat of a screaming ambulance as it hurtled down the highway from DeKalb to Chicago, cutting a swath through the traffic and scattering the cars like toys on the right and left. At other times, friends drove me the hundred miles to the Chicago hospitals, because I didn't drive, and I would return to DeKalb exhausted every night. John was uncomplaining and nearly always cheerful. Neither of us could believe that he was dying. I guess we didn't want to believe it, and there was always hope for a miracle. We both believed in and had faith in God, and we trusted Him with all our hearts. John would ask, "Do you think I'm going to make it?" and I would reply, "Of course you're going to make it. We've come through worse than this," referring to his heart operation. He lived out the last month of his life at Kindred Hospital in Sycamore, Illinois, about eight miles from DeKalb. He suffered no pain, but he was helpless, bedridden, and the doctors told me that, if he lived, he would become an invalid. John died peacefully on July 6, 2004.

I had to decide what to do about a funeral. A few years before, we had had a discussion in which he was reluctant to participate. My own desire is to be cremated, but he resisted that idea. Finally, I caught on and said, "John, do you want a big, old-fashioned Finnish-style funeral with the body present, a church service, flowers, lots of people, food, and burial in the cemetery?" He looked relieved. So, when the time came, I arranged a big funeral. The church was packed, there were words of remembrance from many people who loved him, and I even arranged for his good Finnish friend, Oscar Forsman, to play John's favourite polka on his accordion.

As I looked at John in his casket, I found myself staring in fascination at his folded hands, as I had stared at my father's hands some forty years earlier. I recalled how John's hands had cupped my face for a gentle kiss, rested reassuringly on my shoulders when I needed comforting, and caressed my body with infinite tenderness.

The day after the funeral, I visited his grave in the cemetery, which stretched endlessly across the flat prairie under an endless blue sky. I finally broke down at the sight of the flower-strewn grave. I wanted to fling myself on the grave just to be close to him. It was all so quiet and so final. I found myself thinking of King Lear's terrible cry over the body of his beloved daughter Cordelia (surely the most tragic cry in all of literature): "Thou'lt come no more, Never, never, never, never, never!"

When I reflected later on what had happened, I remembered that, when my mother died, I had hoped that wherever she was, there would be tea and poetry. As for John, wherever he is, I hope that there are polka bands and classes to teach. His colleagues described him as an "exemplary professor and student advocate." When asked about his legacy in an interview conducted some months before his demise, John replied simply, "I would like people to remember that I cared about students."

I was devastated by John's death and the terrible, terrible silence that followed. How could God allow a much-needed person to leave this world? There is so much we don't understand. I had to deal with disbelief, as most people do, and the wrenching realization that not only had a person died, but that an era had come to an end and that life would never be the same again. I wanted to echo Heathcliff's words after Cathy's death: "Haunt me, then! Drive me mad! only do not leave me in this abyss, where I cannot find you!" I was grateful for the support of family and friends, but this struggle is essentially a lonely one. I cried rivers of tears, even as I felt somewhat ashamed about not dealing with the situation more rationally. But, finally, I came to be grateful that we had enjoyed 35 years together and that John had gone at the height of his powers, heaped with honours, at the close of a 50-year career, doing work he loved. This response may be regarded by some as a rationalization, but I am mindful of something my brother Tom once said: "I hope I have the sense to retire when people are still saying, 'What a great teacher! We're going to miss him,' instead of saying, 'Why doesn't he retire? Doesn't he know that he's lost his edge?'"

In the year following John's death, I found myself swamped with bills from doctors and hospitals, and I had to deal extensively with insurance companies and the university concerning pension payments and other benefits. A dear friend who was astute in matters of business came to help me with innumerable forms to be completed and with endless telephone calls. I came to welcome these diversions in the face of overwhelming grief. We went out for lunch two days a week, and I welcomed the company. Gradually, I came to realise that I had to think seriously about the unthinkable—life without John. What to do! Basically, I had to decide whether to remain in DeKalb or to move back to Vancouver. The argument for remaining in DeKalb was powerful. In the thirty years we had spent there, I had put down some roots, I liked the area, especially its proximity to Chicago. Also, I had established friendships, and I was involved in church and community activities. The argument for returning to Vancouver was also powerful. I knew the area well from my ten-year residence there while teaching at UBC, and I had family there, consisting of my sister-in-law, two nieces, a nephew, one great-niece and three great-nephews. I had many misgivings, but I finally decided to return to Vancouver. I also decided to enter a retirement home, so that my family wouldn't worry about me.

During this difficult period, I was sustained by my study of the Bible and by my beloved poets. All my life, I have tried to make and hold onto a connection with God, however dire the circumstances. Faith in God was, to me, from my childhood, as natural as breathing. In difficult situations, I turned to God and asked for help. It always came in one form or another. Sometimes it took the form of a comforting word or a hug from a friend or relative. I confess that I have not always been true to this guide. In moments of extreme grief over John's death, I became angry with God for taking away my beloved companion. But I recovered. Surely, I thought, the same force, the super intelligence that holds the earth in its orbit and keeps the stars in their courses will guide our lives, however dimly it is hidden in the mists of time and space. I identified with Jane Fonda, who declared, in a recent television interview, that, after being raised as an atheist, she had found God. She felt that she is being "guided" in her life, and she reported experiencing some miracles. I believe in miracles, too, convinced that they prove the existence of an hitherto unsuspected law. This law is higher, far higher, than the troubles, the petty concerns, the strife that consumes our world.

The Bible is a very practical guide that is often overlooked, often subscribed to with little understanding or conviction. Actually, the Bible, especially the Psalms, is full of promises of direction, protection, and deliverance. I have learned to trust these promises, to make them my own by filling my thoughts with them. A favourite verse that I have often clung to, when fear tries to creep in, is this one from Isaiah 43:

When thou passest through the waters, I will be with thee; and through the rivers, they shall not overflow thee: when thou walkest through the fire, thou shall not be burned; neither shall the flame kindle upon thee.

Among the poets, I have found many references to immortality. I think that many people who have lost a dearly loved one find consolation in the promise that there will be a reunion after death. I am personally sustained by my conviction of immortality, the certainty that John and I will meet again in some better place. Elizabeth Barrett Browning wrote: "I love thee with the breath, Smiles, tears of all my life! - and, if God choose, I shall but love thee better after death." And Robert Browning proclaimed:

Then a light, then thy breast,
O thou soul of my soul! I shall clasp thee again,
And with God be the rest!

# Chapter 10

I AM COMING to the end of this memoir. I am 87, and I have lost those nearest and dearest to me—my husband, my parents, my brother, and several close friends. As a result of these profound losses, I understand and am experiencing, for the first time, what T.S. Eliot meant by "partly living." However, I am grateful for the loving companionship of my sister-in-law Doreen, my three nieces, and my nephew. I live in a retirement home now, and I am legally blind, a condition that began almost ten years ago and has worsened since John's death. It has deprived me of my reading vision, which is a hardship for a once voracious reader.

My sight problem really began when I was about twelve years old. It has been a lion in my path all my life. In my childhood, some eye doctors did not believe in prescribing lenses that would bring a shortsighted child's vision to normal, or near normal, the theory being that this would make the eyes too dependent on those lenses. The result was that many children, like myself, struggled to see the world clearly, especially the school blackboards. I was too proud to ask to be moved to the front of the classroom, and so I suffered. When eventually I did get glasses at the age of twelve, I felt very self-conscious, as few children wore glasses in those days. As I grew older, the problem intensified.

But, when I moved to Vancouver in 1965 to become a professor at UBC, I found an ophthalmologist who introduced me to contact lenses. What a wonderful discovery! They transformed my life. The whole world sprang into sharp focus and vivid colour, clearer and more brilliant than I had ever imagined it. But this happy circumstance didn't last, and my sight began once more to deteriorate. At the time, John was troubled, but his response was reassuring: "Don't worry about a thing. I'll be your eyes."

These days I manage my life quite well, once places become familiar to me, albeit with some difficulty. I can shop, do my banking, and go for walks. But, in new surroundings with which I have not familiarized myself, I am lost. The lesson is, I suppose, that memory is an important factor in seeing.

In completing a memoir, there is always a temptation to draw a moral, to offer advice, or to fall back on a platitude. As the memoir shows, I made many changes over the years. Yes, I was often frightened. Yes, I feared failure, as we all do. But failure isn't so bad, unless we refuse to learn from it and continue making old mistakes. And, yes, I sometimes wondered whether I had done the right thing.

But, as the memoir illustrates, I decided that, since I had only one life to live, I would make it as interesting, even exciting, as possible. I knew that such a course would involve risks, perhaps even plunge me into despair. And yes, I might have ended up living in a hovel, with barely enough to eat. But that course was, I decided, better than becoming bored.

I might point out that I had no special privileges. I grew up poor in a world that offered very limited opportunities, especially for women. But I chose to use what I had in my hands, to control my life as much as possible, and you can, too. It takes courage, faith, and persistence.

There is a temptation to accept a job when you are young and fresh out of high school or college. The most alluring aspect is the money that enables you to indulge yourself in ways that please you. The danger is that you might elect to remain in that job, as the years pass, because the pay is good and the conditions comfortable. Soon you will find yourself with ten to fifteen years invested in a company pension, and the urge is strong to stay where you are, even if you find more than a few aspects downright tedious, or if the administration is not to your liking. You might even feel under-appreciated. Yet you remain in place, hostage to your pension, largely out of caution, or even fear, about making a change. Sometimes excuses present themselves—"I'm too young," or "I'm too old," or "I haven't the experience, the education, or the confidence."

It must be remembered that seeking our freedom does involve responsibility. In my case, I sought my freedom, but I made sure that I had the resources along the way. At each stage, I cashed in my pension money to finance a new adventure, and I never looked back. In all, I surrendered 24 years of pension money. I could have stayed in these jobs. I didn't hate any of them. In fact, I enjoyed some aspects of my work. I am not denying the need for a pension to provide you with security in old age, but I question the wisdom of planning your future completely around an expected pension and letting it govern your life. It can be a hindrance to great enterprises. I know a few people who can't wait to retire to do, they say, the things they really want to do. To me, the sad implication is that they have spent the best years of their lives, the years when their health and energy level are at their peak, in jobs that, at best, they tolerate, and, at worst, they hate.

The comparison I make is between launching into turbulent waters, with danger on every side, or contenting oneself with floating idly in a placid pond. I chose the first course, and found it exhilarating. At least I knew I was alive! Had I not launched out into those turbulent waters, I would not have found the exciting, life-changing experiences that brought me much reward. I would not have found the real calling I discovered as a teacher, and I wouldn't have met John.

Now you may say, "But I don't know what I want to do! I really have no special driving interest to pursue." My answer is: how do you know unless you try different paths? How do you know they won't lead to an exciting new life, one that will bring fulfillment beyond your dreams? Remember that the happiest people are those who have a passion for what they do. Such people are rare. Most of us settle for so much less than we might achieve. I truly believe, with Browning, that "a man's reach should exceed his grasp—else what's a heaven for?"

I am concluding this memoir by addressing some questions to those people (and I think they may be numerous) who yearn to make significant life changes.

Are you being held hostage to a pension?

Do you realise that, by waiting until retirement to do the things that really interest you, you are perhaps postponing happiness and deferring fulfillment?

Have you considered that, by the time you reach retirement, you may not have the health or the energy level to pursue your interests? Or that you might have responsibilities, such as looking after an aging parent or a child?

Have you the courage and the faith to make life-changing decisions and carry them out?